D0392715

Esther

A True First Lady

Dianne Tidball

Christian Focus Publications

© Copyright Dianne Tidball 2001
ISBN 1-85792-671-4

Published in 2001
by
Christian Focus Publications, Geanies House, Fearn
Ross-shire, IV20 1TW, Great Britain

www.christianfocus.com

Printed and bound in Great Britain by
Cox & Wyman, Reading, Berkshire

Cover design by Alister MacInnes

Cover photo by Fin MacRae
e-mail: finmacrae@photograph.net

To Derek and Richard for their love and support.
To the congregation at Ruislip Baptist Church for their
encouragement and enthusiasm for our studies in
Esther.

CONCORDIA UNIVERSITY LIBRARY
PORTLAND, OR 97211

UNIVERSITY LIBRARY
ENGLAND D.C. 27706

Contents

1

Esther – a Post-Feminist Icon?

At the beginning of the twenty-first century women and men find themselves in a world which is post many things: post-Christian, post-modern, post-evangelical and, many would consider, post-feminist. How should we as Christians react to the community around us and is it possible to find God in the midst of all the topsy-turvy values and belief in nothing or anything?

The book of Esther gives us a way of viewing our world and seeing that God is at work even in the most secular of communities and in the most godless circumstances. There are lessons to be learned from some great Biblical heroes of the past, Esther and Mordecai who lived, loved, had faith and took courage in an empire that did not acknowledge God as we know him and which behaved in a way that makes many of our scandals today seem tame.

In the opening chapter of the book we will meet Queen Vashti, a feminist icon, because she dared to take a stand against a male-dominated oppressive regime. She was courageous and had an integrity that is impressive. She took a stand for women's rights so much so that a law had to be passed against her to ensure that all the other wives in the empire didn't follow her example.

However, Esther, by comparison, is a post-feminist icon. She did not fight the patriarchal system, she did not attempt to win rights for women or make a stand for gender issues, for that she disappoints some feminist theologians. She worked within a corrupt and debauched society, winning friends and influencing people and never losing her vision of God or her humility. From a position within the system God used her to save his people. She would never have burned her bra, taken legal action against harassment or campaigned for the vote. She would never have had the opportunity. She used her status as the Queen to save her people, she risked everything in so doing, she is an icon because she is a role model of how it is possible to live and work within a godless system and be a channel of his grace allowing his purposes to be fulfilled.

You may read this book and decide you prefer Vashti to Esther or vice versa. Alternatively they may both speak to you of a way of living that is radical because it is uncompromising. Some Christians find themselves having to submit to social structures that are unjust and debauched and they choose to play along with that culture in order to achieve glory for God. Some Christians find themselves fighting social cultures because they are unjust and debauched and do so to achieve the glory of God. Neither is better than the other, God leads us differently and God directs us in a variety of ways to fulfil his purposes.

2

Ancient Story, Modern Application

Are you ready for some surprises? What follows is not what you might anticipate from Biblical history, it is more of a soap opera or a melodrama. Like many soap operas, this is a story of strong ambitious men, beautiful intelligent women, groups vying for power and control. There are threats of death, enormous risks taken, genocide, ethnic cleansing, self-sacrifice, evil forces and good triumphing in the end. It could be Jeffrey Archer's latest thriller or a Barbara Cartland romance spiced up a bit. There are characters who reflect greed, power, prejudice and arrogance, who manipulate and oppress others in order to massage their fragile vanity. There are others who are people of integrity and dignity, who have courage and are honest, who take risks for what matters, who are self-effacing and modest.

We don't expect this in a book of the Bible. Seemingly worse is that the Book of Esther does not mention God at all and the context is the complete opposite to that of political correctness by contemporary standards. It is a story of women who are groomed for a year to be good enough for a night with the King, of a Queen selected for her beauty, of women having no say in their destiny, used as playthings of their masters, kept in their place, not allowed to question their husbands or appear disrespectful.

It is the story of the young and innocent Esther, the evil Haman and the astonishing Mordecai. It is written in an age so different from our own that it is not immediately apparent how it can have anything to say to us today. Yet the characters and events have been repeated numerous times throughout history and the lessons of this astounding narrative are as relevant today as they were 2,500 years ago when the events were first recorded.

Whether we are male or female, ugly or beautiful, powerful, weak, poor or rich this book points us to a way of living that is radical, dangerous, controversial and yet also noble, holy and admirable.

History, fiction or wisdom tale

There have been a number of recent Old Testament historians who have struggled to accept the events of Esther as historical. This is a pity and suggests a starting point of doubt rather than a rational weighing of the evidence. The Histories written by the Greek historian Herodotus, cover a great number of events contemporary with the happenings of Esther without actually mentioning Esther or Mordecai. This does not mean the events of Esther did not exist but that they were not known of by a far away

Greek historian and were not relevant to his purposes. The whole background of Esther rings true to what we know of ancient Persian culture, much of the social information and cultural practices are supported by Herodotus. The existence of the harem, the political success of a huge empire and the luxurious trappings of the Palace are just a few examples of parallels found in Esther and in secular writing.

The writer of Esther is not interested only in writing what happened. He has a purpose beyond recording the events of history and is seeking to convey truths about God, his providence, his people and the origins of the festival of Purim (explained in chapter 9). Purim has no basis in Jewish Law, it is not mentioned in Leviticus or Deuteronomy and so one purpose of Esther is to justify and explain the feast of Purim. Esther 'authorises Purim's continuation' as Bernard Anderson[1] says. Some have argued that Esther is only a festival legend or a historicised wisdom tale. In other words it is a story that has been fabricated to support a festival or it is a parable or wise fable that has been loosely connected to a historical setting. While both of these have some credence there is no reason why the book of Esther should not be fully historical with elements of it being used in a festive setting with a meaning and significance to instruct and inform.

Amongst scholars, opposition to Esther abounds

and scepticism is rampant for a variety of reasons. It is the only Old Testament Book not found amongst the Dead Sea Scrolls and the ancient Talmudic scholars questioned whether reading Esther 'defiled the hands'. Anderson argued that it had no theological value describing it as, 'an uninviting wilderness' and contrasting it with the 'frequent oases of inspired Scripture'. I do recognise where these learned people are coming from but I would suggest that they have missed the point of what is an intensely secular book, included in the canon of Scripture for the majority of God's people who live and work in a secular community. It is rich in teaching and lessons for all because it appears to hang so loosely to the devoutly religious and pious works that we think of as spiritual.

Where it all happened

The events took place in the land of Persia, what we know today as Iran, during the years 486–465 BC. King Xerxes, son of Darius III, was on the throne, and ruled over a huge empire centred on the capital Susa. His empire stretched from India to Egypt including as far south as Ethiopia and as far west as the Eastern Mediterranean. He ruled with absolute power, in other words no one could question him, he could order anything and his command would be carried out. No-one was permitted to enter his presence without being invited. If they did they risked being punished by death unless the golden sceptre was held out to them which would indicate the King would accept their interruption.

The author

With little conclusive evidence of who wrote Esther it is traditionally ascribed to Mordecai. In 9:20 and 32 there is a suggestion that the book was written by Mordecai along with letters to explain the Feast of Purim and to encourage and inspire the Jewish nation. The Talmud claims that it was written by the 'men of the Great Synagogue', but this is not a convincing claim because it is so general and it is difficult to support with any evidence. Others have suggested it was written by an unknown author from Persia, possibly Susa, who knew of the traditions of the Persian court, who was Jewish but who was not closely associated with the Jerusalem traditions and not absorbed by God's dealings with Israel. If it is a person marginalised from the apparent mainstream of Jewish life, Mordecai fits the description of such an author admirably.

3

What a party!

Esther chapter 1

As the Book of Esther opens we are immediately launched into the historical context of the events that follow. Xerxes was king of the Mesopotamian empire. He reigned over a vast area from the Eastern Mediterranean to India. He was delighted with his achievements, the prosperity and the success. He wanted to celebrate all he had done. Xerxes was not a Puritan in any sense of the word – he would make Donald Trump look quite frugal. He based his celebrations in his palace in Susa where for 180 days he displayed his wealth, showed his power, presented his achievements and carried out his ritual. He invited all of the foreign nobles, all those who were important in his 127 provinces, to share in this extraordinary celebration. It is difficult to imagine how they sustained such a long period of celebration.

He followed the six months of exhibiting his success to his leaders and aristocracy from afar, with a banquet lasting seven days for the more important local people. Many of us would be left reeling at the thought of the stamina required to keep going for seven days of banqueting! The excesses involved in seven days of indulgence make our over-consumption appear minor.

Reading through verses 1-8 there is a dazzling portrayal of all the most sparkling, glittering and luxurious in the ancient near eastern world: the finest fabrics from across the whole empire, precious stones including pearl paving the floors, extravagant food and costly wines to each individual's preferred taste. Precious metals were there in abundance, the goblets were made of gold, the couches of silver and gold and furnishings of the finest linen on marble pillars. It all speaks of an opulence and a splendour that we can hardly imagine.

It appears that middle eastern leaders have not changed their style too much. Extravagant and ostentatious displays of wealth are a feature of every generation. The Aga Khan in September 1998 held a huge banquet to celebrate his second marriage, inviting a range of world leaders including the British Foreign Secretary, Robin Cook. The party he threw was of unrivalled extravagance, with a lavish dinner, fireworks and a ball. The Aga Khan, who received his weight in gold, platinum and diamonds from his followers–the four million Ismaili Muslims when he acceded to power–generously gave the Foreign Secretary a steel-and-gold clock and his wife a silver perfume spray.

Queen Vashti, the wife of Xerxes, had her own

banquet so that the women were not left out. It was unlikely to have been on quite the scale of the King's banquet. Nevertheless it is also unlikely that any of the guests went without or found themselves hungry or thirsty.

Many of us think that indulgence and displaying wealth and acquiring status symbols of a material kind is a peculiarly modern phenomenon. However, the exhibition of such riches and the desire to impress by our accumulated things is a feature of humankind since the beginning of time. We so easily fall into the trap of wanting to show off, wanting to impress by what we have rather than focusing on the qualities which last longer.

We may be concerned today that the current generation seems to spend so much time worshipping the idol of pleasure and enjoyment. However, we quickly realise that indulging physical and material appetites has been a major goal of a large proportion of every generation. There is nothing new in wanting to earn as much as possible in as short a time as possible so that the maximum amount of pleasure might be enjoyed. Whether it is nightclubs, sport, hobbies, socialising, drinking, dancing and making merry—it has mostly all been done before. It is just that these days modern technological developments give the opportunity for much greater pleasure seeking, everything from hang gliding to Internet browsing, football following to wide musical experiences. This gives us some optimism that our generation is neither better nor worse than its predecessors.

Command performance refused (1:10-22)

After so many days and months of celebrations King Xerxes was in high spirits – drunk, or at least a little the worse for wear as far as alcohol was concerned. In this state of exuberance he commanded his wife Vashti to appear before him in front of all his male guests. He wanted to show off his beautiful wife, to prove that not only did he have all the material possessions that his subjects could only dream of but also he had the most beautiful woman in the land. He wanted to parade her as a kind of trophy babe. He had no sensitivity to his wife's feelings in this matter. He wanted to display his wife in all her royal finery to a room of boorish men where she would be unlikely to receive the respect and dignity due a woman of her position.

Xerxes might have been King with absolute power but even so his command was culturally shocking. This was a society where women remained heavily veiled in public and no-one would see the features of a woman except her husband. What the King was requesting was appalling to all who valued standards of propriety and decency. I think it unlikely, but there are some who have written about Vashti, claiming that what the King was actually commanding was far worse. That she should appear with only her royal crown on (v. 11) which would have been an indescribable outrage. Whatever the precise details of the King's request it was an offence and a scandal to Vashti.

For Vashti to be paraded before a room full of men would have been a torture – to display her as simply a toy or, let's be clear, a sexual plaything, would have been a horror. There would have been the prospect of leering glances, obscene gestures and crude remarks. Men together, when the alcohol has been flowing freely for seven days, would not be concerned about the honour of the Queen. If the King wanted to show his wife off in such circumstances then the experience for the Queen is not difficult to imagine.

Just recently we had the misfortune to travel with a group of men who were on a stag weekend. We were travelling from Waterloo, London to Brussels by train and so were they. On the outgoing journey they were lively, they stayed in the buffet and for other passengers journeying with them, they were little more than irritating, loud and merry. On the return journey three days later, after seventy-two hours of solid drinking sessions, the story was quite different. They were threatening, offensive and intimidating. They would not be reasoned with and could not be quietened. Anyone who went to the buffet car did so with some fear and trepidation.

They were subjected to verbal abuse and crude gestures. We should not think that the order to Queen Vashti to appear before the King under such circumstances did other than fill her with anxiety and apprehension.

To disobey the King was a monumental decision but this was the choice that Vashti made. She weighed her options and made her choice. It was either an act of great courage or great stupidity, for the King had divine rights, his word was law and he could order people to be killed just for entering his presence without permission. Knowing all this, her refusal to obey his order when he was in high spirits and unlikely to be reasonable, was tantamount to suicide. The insult and the offence to the King would have been obvious to all. Despite the fact that she faced a much worse insult and a greater offence, he was the King and the balance of power was most definitely in his favour. A public rebuff with all his most important advisers and courtiers was a great affront.

Throughout her reign Queen Vashti would have suffered enormous restrictions. She would have kept to royal protocol, followed all the rules and regulations of the court, and been at the beck and call of the King. Maybe this incident, the command from the King was the straw that broke the camel's back. She had all that money could buy, living in luxury and decadence and yet without any trusted companion, close friends or what we would understand as mutual love. She lived in a world of high expectations but pitiful satisfaction. Her social diary promised everything, yet did not seem to deliver.

There are parallels to Diana Princess of Wales. She was one of the most beautiful in the world, having everything that others dream of materially, having access to the most significant people politically, artistically and educationally, being able to visit the most varied and fascinating of places – and yet she was deeply depressed and unhappy at the lack of satisfying relationships and of doing what was required without support, affection or appreciation.

When Queen Vashti refused the King's command clearly Xerxes' pride took a severe battering and his anger was as much at the affront to his own ego as an outrage against Vashti. The King shows himself to be a powerful fool, who has to learn the hard way to value the people whom he should really have valued, rather than all the 'yes men' with whom he had surrounded himself.

The response to Queen Vashti's act of defiance was immediate but not quite the reaction we might have expected. I would have anticipated that Queen Vashti herself would have been severely censured and punished, possibly put to death. That did not happen. But the reaction of the lawyers and officials is intriguing. The outcry was not focused simply on Vashti even though her behaviour was seen as an act of flagrant incitement likely to provoke the nation's women to a kind of marital mutiny. There was an hysterical outcry that she had somehow upset the social structure. It would appear that Mesopotamian society was at a point of social upheaval and that they were experiencing tensions about roles. It would seem that the men expected the women to be submissive and the women's role was to be acquiescent, accommodating and subservient.

Possibly there was some realisation that the women had a just case, that Vashti was right to make a stand but the men were petrified of the consequences. Petticoat power was seen as too dangerous and Girl Power was not a social phenomenon they were prepared to entertain. So the edict was passed that Queen Vashti would not be allowed to enter the King's presence ever again. She either got off lightly or she got all she wanted. This could have been the reward she waited for, to be rid of the suffocating role and to be able to be ordinary again.

We tend to think that the issue of women's rights is a modern concern. The Pankhursts, the campaign for women in ministry, female education, equal pay, equal opportunities in the work place; all seemingly twentieth century battles. Yet the issue of the role of women in society and in the family goes back thousands of years. For King Xerxes and his nobles the matter was settled with a kingdom-wide proclamation that every man should be ruler over his own household, which is interesting in itself.

The passing of a decree to control social relationships ought to give us cause for concern or maybe cynical humour. A law that requires us to respect others is doomed to failure, because if laws have to be passed then the respect is not due since it has not been earned and is an imposition. As a spiritual principle it is right to aim for love and respect within marriage but that principle is difficult to uphold if there is no basis for the respect and no aspect of the relationship that warrants respect. A dutiful obedience can be imposed but respect is a matter of honouring people because they are deserving of it, not forcing a respect against the will. I obey a police officer because of the uniform but I can only respect him or her as a person if they carry out their duties in a way that commands respect.

Interestingly, passing laws about respect is not only an ancient folly. On 7th July 1999 the Louisiana state effected a law that required young people to show respect for their teachers. Pupils must address their teachers and other school employees as 'sir' or 'ma'am'. The Governor, Mike Foster, justified the approach by arguing that respect should be taught at home, but when it wasn't then the schools had to step in. The law applies to all children under ten and laws covering older ages would be phased in, in the future. There are severe reservations held by many as to whether it is possible to change an attitude by the law. The law is important in moulding people's thinking and is significant in the effect it has on social values. For example, when divorce is made easier people's commitment to marriage is reduced. A law demanding respect may have a measure of success, but in the long term, if it is important to change the way people think and their attitudes, then a law alone is inadequate - the law will be seen as a joke and the whole legal process will be undermined. Good laws make sense and are commonly agreed on. If people are worthy of respect and command respect they will receive it, if people are undeserving of respect then no law is going to make people admire them.

The men of the time were left looking foolish if they needed an edict from the King that 'every man should be ruler in his own household' (1:22). The confidence with which the lawyers proclaim that when this decree is proclaimed 'all the women will respect their husbands, from the least to the greatest' is optimistic. If a woman had no respect for her husband before the decree then she is unlikely to suddenly become respectful and submissive because a law says she should. The male and female psyche is much more complex and sophisticated than this and we should recognise that respect is due but it is an attitude of the heart that legislation can do little to alter.

The so-called battle of the sexes is a sad reminder that we live in a fallen world. It's not the way God intended relationships when He created the world. When we look at Genesis 3:16-19 we see that it was when sin entered the world at the Fall that a wedge was driven between men and women and that the perfect relationship God had given to Adam and Eve became flawed. There was gender rivalry, power broking in domestic relationships and the introduction of male dominance and female resistance. However, the amazing thing is that in Christ all things are made new, even the relationships between men and women. As Galatians 3:28 says: 'There is neither Jew nor Greek, slave nor free, male nor female for you are all one in Christ.'

I know that even as Christians, men and women can and do approach things differently. We may communicate differently; we may have different priorities. You only have to read John Gray's *'Men are from Mars, Women are from Venus'*[2] to know this. However, in Christ we have unity, we have the potential and the power to overcome the tensions that are so destructive in our society as they were

29

damaging in the society of Xerxes. Both men and women are demeaned and disadvantaged by the so-called gender wars. Women have made many advances in the twentieth century as far as equal opportunities are concerned, although there may still be a way to go. However, many men have been left confused and marginalised by 'Girl Power', Feminism and the freedom that previous generations of women could never imagine. Many men are left wondering whether they have a role. The feminist hype is in danger of writing off males as irrelevant both economically and domestically. Such opinions destroy the self-esteem of many. This is not God's plan for humanity. God has a significant role for each individual and gives them unique value.

So — was Vashti a martyr to the cause or a fool to herself? She knew the consequences of disobeying the King and yet she was determined to carry through her decision. This is a recurring theme within the book of Esther. She understood what she was doing, yet she was prepared to make a stand. She would be demeaned, humiliated and compromised no more.

When we make decisions we do need to understand the consequences of what we are doing; we should expect to pay the price. If the compromise we are asked to make or the action that is expected of us sits uneasily with our conscience or beliefs, then these are times to take a stand but we do have to accept what comes our way. It is easy to take the moral high ground some might say: what is difficult is paying the price and accepting the consequences that go with it. It may be in our work or in relationships, it may be over money or it may be over ethical issues, but, like Vashti there comes a point when we have to refuse to obey a corrupt or offensive system any further. However, we cannot expect just because we are right that God will protect us from the consequences of our decisions. God will give us the grace to see it through, but we must take our stand aware of the difficulties that could follow.

For many of us Vashti is a courageous example of knowing where to draw the line and having the 'bottle' to do what is right. Too many of us keep giving in to what is going on around us. If we keep on bending to the demands and expectations of others eventually we will be broken and we will have no principles or faith left. If we keep bending to every request that is made, and compromise on every corner then our lives will not reflect the Jesus who died for us. For Queen Vashti holding to her principles cost her her crown, her role, her relationship with the King.

Before we leave Vashti I would like to reflect on one further issue. Vashti might have benefited from the diplomacy of her successor, Esther. She might have shown a little more gracious tact managing the situation more sensitively, avoiding the showdown but ensuring that the King was not humiliated and did not lose face. She might then have maintained the role to which she had become accustomed. An excuse of some kind (ask any secondary school student who hasn't done their homework and they will give a list of well-rehearsed excuses which are almost impossible to refute) — headache, bad hair day, nothing to wear, could have given her adequate escape from the problematic circumstances she faced. However, her actions on such a public occasion with so many important guests were bound to have a significance way beyond more routine refusals of the King.

Down the ages women have achieved great things for God by their acceptance of the social structure and their adaptation to circumstances. Fighting issues head on may have the appearance of great integrity and at times it is essential and heroic but may achieve less for God's kingdom in the long term. Don't forget Jesus' teaching 'Be as shrewd as snakes and as innocent as doves' (Matt. 10:16).

Vashti may be seen as a feminist icon. She dared to stand against the pervasive stereotype of women in her time and many would agree she did the correct thing, making no compromises. For others she is a heroine but they may choose to live their lives differently.

There is a tension between when to compromise and when to make a stand. Vashti did the right thing but that does not always mean it is right for us on every occasion to be uncompromising on every point. We should choose our battles carefully and prayerfully, knowing the ones that really matter and being ready to take the consequences.

A change of heart? (2:1)

Later Xerxes recollected the events that had taken place. The implications of the comment 'he remembered Vashti and what she had done and what he had decreed about her', is that Xerxes regretted his impulsive behaviour. His anger had subsided and in the cold light of day his ruthless treatment of Vashti seemed mistaken and a personal loss. Vashti was both beautiful and the Queen he loved. But the law had been passed and he could not go back on his own word – he had to maintain his role.

It is a considerable irony that one of the greatest kings, whose word was law, whose law was absolute, who had enormous wealth and incredible power, could not acquit his wife when he had formulated a law against her which he subsequently regretted, because he had been drunk at the time.

It only made him look a fool. A king may have considerable power and live in great luxury but his actual control over events may be limited. Those who seem to be able to do just as they please are in fact limited by their own egos and the political structures with which they are surrounded.

It is reminiscent of a later event when Herod made a foolish and thoughtless promise to Herodias' daughter who had charmed him (Matt. 14:6-12). Another man of great power and influence; but because he had made a promise, and the daughter had required the head of John the Baptist, he gave himself no option but to deliver. With much sad regret and recognition that this was a wrong path to pursue, he did not have the strength of character to refute his own promise and find a witty or wise way out of the situation.

This first section of the book of Esther has set the scene for the deliverance of God's people through the courage, integrity and duty of both Esther and Mordecai. However, before we leave the first chapter let us reflect on some of the issues that have been raised.

• The danger of excesses are indicated. Any actions, decisions, discussions which take place under artificial influences or with the goading and excitement of others may not seem so wise or sensible in the cold light of day. For us this is a spiritual issue. If we are to be God's people and stand out as different we should not share the overindulgence and excesses of some of those around us. Lack of restraint is sin in itself but it may also lead to more serious consequences than at first thought. It may seem like fun at the time but the repercussions may leave the apparent jollity looking rather tawdry. There are many New Testament references to being 'not lovers of wine' (Titus 2:3) and being temperate. It doesn't mean that as Christians we are expected to be boring but it does mean that the fullness of life that we enjoy in Christ is not lived at someone else's expense but actually to other people's benefit.

• God's intention for men and women is for mutual support and compatibility. We see from the book of Esther the breakdown of God's original intention and the working out of the Fall: fractured relationships, unhelpful laws imposing respect, and requirements made of individuals inappropriately. That is not what God intended. He intends a mutual respect and submission, and an awareness of each other as people, not as possessions or sex objects.

• There are times when it is right to refuse to conform, to obey the rules, to do what is expected or required. When we take a stand we must do so with our eyes open to the consequences and we must accept those consequences whatever they are because this is not a perfect world. It is a world where those who do what is right, who act with integrity, will at times be vilified and derided, but we must do what we know we are called to do.

King Xerxes

King Xerxes was a colourful and eccentric individual who is written about at some length in *The Histories of Herodotus*. One of Xerxes' most memorable exploits was his attempt to take Greece. This may well have been just before Esther became Queen. Across the waters of the Hellespont he constructed two bridges out of boats to allow his armies to pass to the West out of Asia. Just as the army was about to proceed, a fierce storm blew up and destroyed the bridges he had built. Xerxes was furious, outraged that the sea should rebel against him. He ordered that the sea be whipped 300 times and that shackles be thrown in to symbolise the sea's subjugation to him. This was duly done. I am not sure how convinced Xerxes was of his power: it would appear from Herodotus' comments about him that only an ego as huge as Xerxes' could have imagined such a ridiculous bridge building exercise to have any chance of success.

The history books speak of Xerxes as one who was troubled by ghostly visits and messages and that his sleep was often fitful. He was at the mercy of signs and dreams, constantly changing his mind, never sure of his own judgement and listening to a variety of different voices never knowing which one was the truth. He never did defeat the Greeks. At the battle of Salamis the Greek navy wiped out the Persian navy and Xerxes retreated to Asia Minor.

Xerxes does not come across as the most favourable of characters. Some have described him as mean and impulsive, lacking judgement and indecisive but there are writings that portray him as bold, ambitious with vision and confidence, once he had risen above his superstition. He was known for his exploits with women, even his brother's wife and daughter. He would have no hesitation in regarding any woman as being for his personal gratification. There is also sad evidence that the king would go to disgraceful lengths of murder and mutilation to satisfy himself.

4

Miss Persia 478 BC

Esther chapter 2

Most of us have the view that the Bible is about holy people leading sanctified lives who walk closely with God and see life from a spiritual perspective. Yet the Bible is actually much more true to life than that. In parts it is really quite raunchy and could even be accused of being suitable only after the 9 p.m. watershed!

It is into a scandalous and tumultuous context that Esther and Mordecai are introduced. The Queen had dared to disobey the King and all of the kingdom knew about it. The King needed a new wife and embarked upon little less than what today would be called serial rape in order to find her.

The search for a new queen (2:2-5)
This section of Esther's story makes many of today's soap operas look like a kindergarten story by comparison. It is steamy stuff not for the fainthearted. This is a situation far removed from ours, with a totally different cultural background and attitude to the young and to women that appals and horrifies us.

The king had no wife since Vashti had been dismissed and so his personal attendants suggested that the most beautiful young virgin women, much younger than the king, be selected, pampered and groomed for him. After a year of preparation and training they would spend the night with Xerxes and in the morning go to the harem in the king's palace. The one that Xerxes liked best he could keep. Xerxes' officials pander to his lecherous tastes. His behaviour, which today would be seen as perverted and criminal, is attested to in some detail in the writings of Herodotus and already mentioned in the previous details about Xerxes.

This is almost too shocking even for our liberated senses at the beginning of the twenty-first century. Young girls, some thirteen, fourteen or fifteen, would have one night of probable terror and then be condemned to what was little better than widowhood in the harem. They would spend the rest of their lives closeted from the outside world and only called by the king occasionally, if that. The opportunities for motherhood and a loving family life were remote. It was an inhuman and demeaning existence. Recent archaeological excavations have revealed the site of the harem showing the rooms where the girls would have lived. This sad slice of history is supported by graphic evidence.

Nowadays Xerxes would probably be arrested and charged with child abuse, serial rape and serious assault. Then it was an accepted part of Mesopotamian life, although the effects on the young lives may have been no less traumatic than such incidents today.

On hearing the suggestion that all the most beautiful girls be lined up for him to choose a queen, the King responds with what must be the master of understatement, — 'this idea appealed to the King'!

A focus on Mordecai and Esther (2:6-7)
Mordecai and Esther were relatives, most likely cousins or second cousins. They were Jewish exiles whose great grandparents had been brought to Susa from Jerusalem in captivity when Nebuchadnezzar was on the throne. Like any displaced people today this was grim although as the generations settled they acclimatised to the new situation. Looking at the Psalms (e.g. 137), we begin to understand the sense of displacement and the refugee mentality which was powerful. Mordecai was missing his homeland and longed to be back at the centre of his nation and faith.

Esther, Mordecai's niece, was a beautiful young girl in her mid-teens. In Hebrew her name was Hadassah or Myrtle meaning divine generosity or peace. Esther has links with the Persian word for star or the Babylonian goddess Ishtar. She was an orphan, and the only background information we have is the mention of her parents being dead and that she is under the care and guardianship of her cousin. As the story of Esther unfolds it is clear that Mordecai has brought Esther up with great integrity. He has prepared her to be faithful and loyal in her religion despite being in a hostile and unsympathetic context. She is beautiful, charming and intelligent with a sensitive ability to deal with people, but Mordecai has also ensured that she has a keen sense of duty, courage and moral responsibility.

His example is a challenge to any of us with responsibility for raising children and giving them a good foundation in life. It is easy these days to focus on educational achievement, excellence in examinations or in sport, and other important activities. But how many of us take equally seriously our fundamental responsibility to raise children with good character and honesty, who are trustworthy, reliable, conscientious, having a sense of spiritual heritage, godly loyalty, discretion, courage, sound values and duty?

Mordecai was a single man, living with the social and emotional turmoil of exile and death in the family. Being in an alien culture meant he was without all the networks of support that might usually have been available to him. In fact throughout the events portrayed in this book, Esther shows an astonishing array of skills and qualities in handling people, problem solving and meeting objectives. She would have all that is needed to be a first class leader and manager today. The book shows Esther as a developing and growing personality. She is not portrayed statically in flat characterisation, but as someone who faces challenges, overcomes fears and confronts new situations. It is a vivid representation of an extraordinary individual.

Those who have studied this book from a feminist perspective struggle with Esther. She appears to represent a type of woman who complies with a male dominated system with all the worst excesses that are possible. She follows a stereotypical female role submitting herself to a pattern of life that can be seen as demeaning and oppressive. She is not then considered by those critics to be a figure whose example should be followed. While I have benefited enormously from feminist perspectives in theology and appreciate the challenging questions that are asked, it is a mistake to disregard Esther because she was in a culture where women did accept a secondary status to men and because there was an oppressive social structure in which she acquiesced. She is a model of leadership, diplomacy, integrity and courage despite the social context in which she is found. While Vashti might find more support among the feminists because of her audacious stand against Xerxes, it was Esther who won the fight for her people.

Into a grubby and not very edifying situation the seemingly saintly Esther and the holy Mordecai are thrust. We shouldn't be so surprised — the church is no stranger to scandal. Scandals occur with unfortunate regularity. You only have to look back over recent years and recall Jimmy Bakker or the Nine o'Clock Service in Sheffield as well as other stories that hit the tabloids with frequent regularity.

A slight diversion but an amusing one. A scandal which stays in the memory as being even more bizarre than most is the story of the Vicar of Stiffkey in Norfolk recorded in Matthew Parris's book, *The Great Unfrocked: Two Thousand Years of Church Scandal*.[3]

The Vicar of Stiffkey had a particular mission or ministry to the call girls of London. He would leave his parish and travel to the metropolis each week seeking to support and bring comfort to young women in a hopeless situation. A commendable ministry we would agree. However, over time the Vicar of Stiffkey became compromised, was accused of being too close to some of the women and engaged in inappropriate ministry.

Eventually he was unfrocked, losing his living despite appealing twice and protesting his innocence. Having run out of funds to defend himself he took a somewhat eccentric path. He became an exhibit in Blackpool, sitting in a barrel on the promenade and charging for a viewing.

In July 1937 he followed the example of Daniel and faced a den of lions, or one lion to be precise. Unlike Daniel he did it out of choice. In Skegness amusement park the Vicar of Stiffkey entered a cage with the friendly passive lion Freddie. From this unique place he denounced the Church of England and all of its leaders.

Unfortunately, one evening Freddie resorted to instinctive behaviour patterns and mauled the Vicar of Stiffkey to death. Harold Davidson died professing his innocence and claiming martyrdom.

Closer to home, less bizarre but no less sad scandals occur. We read with frequent regularity of Christian leaders caught in immorality, dishonesty or cases of abuse. We are convinced that irreparable damage is done to God's kingdom but God knows the human heart much better than we do. Such scandals have happened in the past and will happen in the future but God mysteriously works out his purposes often despite them and sometimes through them.

It is curious to see God's purposes working out in such circumstances. It is just a little surprising that the godly Mordecai allowed Esther to be selected for such a future. We don't know whether he could have hidden her or sent her away but as part of God's purposes Esther is drawn into this royal court of decadence and dubious morality.

Persian beauty treatment
fit for a queen (2:8-9)

Esther was chosen as one of the young women to be prepared for the King. She entered the royal household under the supervision of Hegai where she was given all the best in facials, toning, massage, skin care and other beauty treatments. She was to become the 450 BC equivalent of Miss World, with all the trappings of privilege and wealth and all the shallowness of a world that values physical attractiveness above all else.

It is all credit to Esther that it is within this context that she maintains her personal priorities and is able to keep a sense of proportion and not think too highly of herself. Many heads would have been turned and many young women would become pretentious and vain under such circumstances.

Esther made a good impression. She pleased the master of the harem, her winsome personality and ability to relate well to people comes through at this early stage of the story. She is given the best place in the harem and allotted seven maids for her personal care, she makes the most of the situation. She shows herself to be teachable, she listens to all that Hegai advises and follows his instructions. Not one to think that she knew it all, Esther is an example to all of us that we should be ready to learn from others since we never know who God might send to support and guide us. In Esther's case it was someone who did not share her religious values and whose counsel she might have felt justified in ignoring.

At this stage of events (verses 10 and 20), Esther chose discretion rather than openness and did not reveal her background or nationality. She kept hidden the fact that she was Jewish. We may want to criticise her for this and suggest she be much more open and clear about her origins. We may wish that she had been a much more candid witness. However she has wisdom and a sense of discernment. She follows the wisdom learnt from the Proverbs, such as 21:23: 'He who guards his mouth and his tongue keeps himself from calamity.' It isn't always helpful to wear our heart on our sleeve about our faith. Our lifestyle should speak louder than any words and when asked we will then have a credible basis for explaining about our faith.

I am not comfortable with people who speak first about being a Christian and then comment upon other issues somewhat piously. I remember watching the TV programme *Kilroy* one morning when the issue under discussion was to do with marriage. One lady who appeared warm and kindly made her contribution by saying: 'As a Christian I believe....' I'm sure she felt that by saying 'as a Christian' she was being a witness and in a way I admire her for doing so, but as soon as she said it I could feel the TV audience inwardly groan and mentally switch off because of how she had opened her comment. What she had to say was good but it was lost because people stereotyped her as religious and somehow not relevant. As if 'she would say that, wouldn't she.' We can often be more influential by being discreet and subtle.

As Christians we should be speaking out on all kinds of issues and take every opportunity to present values and opinions that are constructive and in line with Biblical teaching. However, we need to do it in a subtle and wise way so that people will listen and be influenced. We should never hide our faith but we do need to be thoughtful and discerning about how we can best present the claims of the Gospel today when people are put off by an overtly religious position.

For a godly woman, Esther found herself in bizarre circumstances full of corruption and power. Mordecai must have worried about her and I suspect some in the community would have been judging her. A young girl in such a powerful place with all those young courtiers and nothing to do each day except to be pampered and entertained. No place for a godly woman. God couldn't possibly use someone in such circumstances.

It happens today as well. Many of God's people do find themselves working in bizarre situations where there is no clear evidence of God at work and plenty of apparent evidence to the contrary. It is easy to question their spirituality or think that they have their guidance wrong. We need to thank God for women and men who are existing in situations that cause us doubts and misgivings. Christian politicians are often criticised for their party allegiance, those in the media like Cliff Richard and Steve Chalke are criticised for the compromises people think they must make. We should be grateful for these people who go in the name of Christ where the rest of us would fear to tread. It is so easy to be critical and so easy to judge.

I have known a Christian working as a photographer for the *Sun*, the newspaper renowned for its photographs of under-dressed women. I have known a range of police officers involved in situations that would give us grave concern about godly values. The armed services, the prison service, social workers, the business world can be tough situations that don't always sit easily with a Christian lifestyle but that is no reason to absent ourselves from them. Don't judge these people. Pray that God will use them in their seemingly compromising situations.

God at work in debauchery, decadence and intrigue (2:12-18)

It strikes home forcefully that here is a situation of utter inequality and decadence where seemingly little of moral strength can be salvaged and yet here God chooses to work out his plans. Through the debauchery of others which caused Queen Vashti to make her stand, God saves His people.

There are so many parallels today that we could mention. How often we have written off situations as too appalling, ungodly or hopeless for God to be at work. I think of a declining Church that had fallen from the 'glory' days of being a packed preaching centre and seemed to have no future. It was written off by some in Christian leadership as one that would die and for whom there was little hope. God blessed that fellowship and today it is one of the largest fellowships in the country.

In Susa, the royal court where no acknowledgement was made of Yahweh, God of all gods, he is working and his plans are coming to fruition. He allows Esther to be a part of this sad social structure. Perhaps we should not be so quick to withdraw from situations which horrify or offend us and be patient enough to see God at work.

Esther and Xerxes

Esther went through with the requirement of giving herself to the King. It would be easy to slide over this because of Christian sensitivities but it really does mean what it says. She slept with the King and was required to please him. It did not mean twin beds and a philosophical discussion about the role of the queen in Mesopotamian life. They had intercourse and Esther would have spent some time in her year of preparation learning how to please and satisfy him. No issue is made by the writer of Esther of the fact that a fastidious Jewish girl would be appalled by intermarriage. Looking at Ezra, written at a similar time to Esther, intermarriage is strictly forbidden (Ezra 9–10). For Esther there must have been huge adjustments in her thinking and expectations. This was not what she had planned for herself and there must have been doubts and confusion, if not direct resistance in her own mind to the situation she found herself in. She must have resolved the conflicts in her mind in some way to present to the king such an attractive personality.

There is no intention of being salacious but this passage reminds us that the Bible is a real book, about real people, in real situations, for real people, living real lives. It is a hard-hitting book. It doesn't pull any punches and it faces up to the issues, such as promiscuous lifestyles that are in our media daily. The Bible has an authentic message but too often that message has been blunted and lost its cutting edge and its ability and power to speak to real people. The blame must lie with the teachers of the Bible who can, with a great number of good intentions, present a cosy, warm story that fails to touch people. It is too easy to gloss over the tough message of the Bible and not allow it to speak to us directly and relevantly about the world in which we live.

A few years ago a book was written about evangelism to men entitled '*Real Men don't eat quiche*'. It argued that real men need real spiritual food, not the quiche version. We can say the same for women. People need the truth, not bland watered down versions of the truth. The real message of the Bible will challenge and penetrate people's lives, the other will just make them sick of an insipid Christian faith that demands little, offers little and pretends that the world is not as it really is.

We are not told how Esther felt or how she coped that night, but she was a huge success. The King fell hopelessly, helplessly and completely for her and made her his queen. An orphaned Jewish girl became queen of the vast Mesopotamian empire. This shows what a magnificent sense of irony God has. Great kingdoms that seem so powerful are mere puppets in the hand of God. (See the note at the end of the chapter on the absence of Esther being mentioned in historical documents.)

The plot thickens (2:19-23)

Like all good thrillers the events of the book of Esther twist and turn unexpectedly. At the end of the second chapter when Esther has been made queen, affairs move on in a fairly incomprehensible manner. Mordecai has remained a faithful and loyal guardian to Esther. He sat at the king's gate of the palace keeping alert to any news of Esther and her well being. It is difficult to imagine a more dedicated and thoughtful guardian.

Joyce Baldwin[4] helpfully explains that to be at the king's gate was to be in the area where justice was dispensed. It is possible that Mordecai, because of his loyalty to Esther, had been promoted to a position such as magistrate. This would have provoked Haman's anger and given Mordecai access to news and conspiracies within the court. It would also have been an ideal position from which to keep a watchful eye on Esther.

Esther herself is also remarkable in her conduct. 'She continued to follow Mordecai's instructions as she had done when he was bringing her up' (2:20). Remember she is now queen, someone with enormous status and influence. It would have been easy for her to kick over the traces and to forget her origins. However, she remains faithful to her upbringing, she shows humility despite her social position, she shows a wisdom beyond her years in keeping to the advice she has been given and the values she has learned from the careful guidance of Mordecai.

While Mordecai was sitting at the king's gate he picked up some local intelligence. He overheard comments and conversations that made him realise that there was a conspiracy to assassinate the king.

Two of the king's officers, Bigthana and Teresh, had become angry about some unstated issue where they felt unjustly dealt with or unappreciated, so they discussed a way of resolving the situation in their favour, no doubt with the intention that one of them, or at least one of their cronies, would take over the throne. They would have been in a better position than most to carry out this act of treachery since they were insiders who had access to the king and a responsibility for his security.

Mordecai, having this information, passed it on to Esther who in turn was able to relay the message to the king. The king was right to be concerned about such conspiracies – they were a real threat and not just an empty possibility. Eventually, in years to come, Xerxes' life ended when he was assassinated in his own palace, one attempt on his life about which he was not forewarned. In verse 22 there are four important little words that endear me to Esther almost more than any other. They are 'giving credit to Mordecai'. As a young bride, in a new social context, needing to prove herself and please her husband, it would have been simple for her to appear to have come by this information herself and to take all the credit herself. She didn't, and that willingness to allow credit to go to the rightful person becomes crucial as God's strategy for saving his people is revealed. Many of us would have been a little selfish, grabbed some of the credit for ourselves and twisted the evidence to put ourselves in a better light. However, if Esther had done that she would not have been able to promote Mordecai's cause so effectively later on.

I once saw the following words on a poster: 'There is no limit to what can be achieved if it doesn't matter who gets the credit.' What a chord that struck. How much we in our churches fail to achieve as a team because some individuals are too keen to gain the credit. How often people fail to act because someone else has stolen their praise in the past. Working as a team is the most effective way to make progress either in the church, in families, at work, in relationships. Sometimes that means we have to be generous with who gets the credit. It will benefit us in the long term but if we take credit that is not due to us then we do untold harm, causing bitterness and mistrust and undermining the ability to work effectively together. Allowing others to take the credit when some of it might come our way is a good discipline to learn. It keeps us humble and aware that all the credit should really go to God anyway.

Esther knew the importance of working in partnership with Mordecai. She didn't know how significant it would be later on that Mordecai got the credit for exposing the conspiracy but it was crucial that he did. The New Testament has a lot to say about working as a body, the business world has in recent years focused on working in a team. There are parallels. It emphasises the need not to be a solo act, and to appreciate the contribution and gifts of others. Working together is so much more productive for God's plans and therefore for everyone's benefit. The strength of each person can be brought to the fore and the weaknesses compensated for by others.

Concluding thoughts on Chapter 2

As we come to the end of the second chapter there are some points I would particularly like to underline. Esther stands out as an amazing young woman in every way. She coped with a situation that might have made other people need psychiatric care. She was attractive physically and in her personality and the kind of person that brought the best out in others. She won the favour of the manager of the harem almost as soon as she had arrived. She endeared herself to all she met. She was a remarkable character who could be used by God for his purposes. Despite all her success she maintained a humility that enabled her to be used.

Mordecai equally is portrayed as a man with enormous dignity and impressive disposition. A man of integrity and wisdom, he had brought Esther up in such a way that she trusted him and followed his guidance. His perseverance, loyalty, willingness to take risks and to allow Esther the freedom to be

God's person for that time, showed him to be a remarkable person.

God's plan unfolds because of the integrity and faithfulness of two people – people who are found worthy of shouldering huge responsibilities. As events move on they are both tested to their limit and found, with God's grace, to be able to cope with the task.

Mordecai had brought Esther up to be true to God whatever the circumstances and not to have her faith undermined by events or the shallow achievements of fame, wealth and political influence. It would be good to think that we are the kind of people who would respond similarly to the events that we face; that we might follow the example of Esther and Mordecai and be people of integrity, loyal to God and winsome to others – people who can be trusted with responsibility in His kingdom. Our ability to do this depends on being willing to give credit to others, to work with others, to have a servant heart and a humble approach when a little power and influence comes our way.

Thank God for Esther and Mordecai. Charles Swindoll is right: 'We desperately need good role models today, not superficial superstars but authentic heroes, people worthy of following –people of integrity who inspire us to do better, climb higher and stand taller.'[5]

Esther in historical documents

There is a historical question that no mention is made of Esther as Queen in the Histories. The queen is named as Amestris. This may indicate that Esther was a second favoured wife or that Amestris became Queen on Esther's death. Chapter 4:11, the fact that she had not been into Xerxes presence for thirty days, may give some credence to the idea of her being a second wife for the king, although it is not possible to be certain and 2:17 suggests something much more than secondary status.

5

The Maggot in the Cherry Pie

Esther chapter 3

Don't you just love it! When everything is going well someone has to come along and spoil it all! It happens in every walk of life, when someone gets a bit too greedy or proud or somehow can't bear everything going so well. There is always a person who will be jealous of others' success and try to undermine it or will not be satisfied with the good times while they last.

Into a happy situation, with a contented king and a beautiful queen, comes the low-life Haman. Haman must have been an excellent politician depending on how you judge such things, or maybe Xerxes displays his lack of judgement again. Having made a terrible blunder over Vashti and having managed to redeem the situation in a way that he didn't deserve with Esther, he continues his pattern of poor decision-making with Haman. The impression given of Haman is that he is a 'yes-man' who had ingratiated himself to Xerxes and managed to deliver results that were pleasing. We will discover much more of Haman as the chapter unfolds. If he had only been a 'yes-man' then it would not have been so bad but he was an evil and corrupt individual whose selfish plans consumed him completely.

Xerxes honoured Haman, giving him a position way above any other in the realm except himself. The king commanded that all the other officials should pay homage to Haman for his achievements and success in office. Haman was an Agagite, a clan of the Amalekites who did not fear God and he reflects perfectly the belief system of his people. They lived by the assumption that chance alone ruled the universe, so it followed that they should do all they could to make chance go their way. They were the original 'me' society. If chance ruled the universe then you had to look out for number one, protecting your own back. They were out to advance their own interests – they would have taken to the National Lottery with huge enthusiasm and had no ethics about making fortune go their way.

That is so like the values and lifestyles presented by much of the media today. Too many people today are out only for themselves and justify it quite openly with no embarrassment or shame. 'If you don't look after yourself no-one else will.' It seems that we are breeding a generation of individualists whose personal ambitions and aspirations are more important than anything else.

Whilst I do not applaud those who resort to anarchist

activities to demonstrate against capitalism and its materialistic greed, I do have sympathy with those who suggest that the way we are living is too costly for many. Those who are successful and do well have affluence and opportunities that they could only have dreamt of a generation ago, but the effect of this rampant materialism, greed and self-indulgence on our communities, is serious. Let's not assume that this is only a problem for the successful – the marginalised are just as capable of greed and self-interest, but they often do not have the power and influence to satisfy such appetites.

Mordecai's response (3:2-5)

We are not sure of the precise reasons why, but Mordecai refused to bow down and honour Haman in the way that everyone else did. It was a matter of principle for Mordecai, although not fully explained by Torah teaching. Jews did bow down to others (1 Sam. 24:8: David prostrating himself before Saul) but Haman was different. Mordecai refused to bow down to Haman because he was an Agagite, a tribe of the Amalekites, an old and bitter enemy of Israel (Exod. 17:8-10: the Amalekites attacked Israel at Rephidim). He may well have bowed down to Xerxes whose office alone commanded respect. Mordecai realised that Haman was not the kind of person worthy of honour and did not want to reinforce false impressions of self-importance and Mordecai would not have wanted to be a hypocrite.

Mordecai was put in a difficult position at this time. Unknown to those around him he was the cousin of the queen and he would not want to make her position unnecessarily difficult, but he was determined to maintain his stand and would not compromise, despite being questioned daily and asked why he would not honour Haman. Interestingly at this stage, Mordecai had not hidden his Jewish background. Part of his argument about why he did not bow to Haman was based on his racial origins so it was important not to hide it. This may seem to be a contradiction of what he had told Esther to do. However, different circumstances require different action and responses. Mordecai was trying to respond with integrity and wisdom in all situations.

Mordecai had already proved his loyalty to the king (2:21-23) so the question of his loyalty to the throne should have been unquestioned. However, Haman does later portray Mordecai as a traitor, just one of the half truths that he puts to Xerxes in trying to get his way. There is, however, a conflict of loyalties. Mordecai by his action puts his whole race in danger although he cannot have known that at the time. There was the tension of being true to his conscience but also loyal to his people. His conscience told him not to bow down to Haman but he would have been unlikely to consciously put his people at such a huge risk. There were probably those around who encouraged Mordecai to loosen up a bit, give a little and just do a pretend bow to Haman to avoid a confrontation. Fortunately, Mordecai was a person of principle who knew what was right and what was wrong. The cost of doing what was right might have seemed far too high, but if Mordecai had not stood up to Haman then he would have got more and more powerful and walked over more and more people.

Around the world today there are people who make heroic stands against injustice and despots. In Burma, Aung San Suu Kyi who won the Nobel Peace prize in her fight for democratic rights spent six years under house arrest, separated from her husband. Nelson Mandela was imprisoned for twenty eight years in his stand against apartheid and will be remembered in history as one of the greatest crusaders for racial equality. In Tiananmen Square, students unsuccessfully made a stand against the lack of freedom, thousands were killed and wounded. There are many others who might have opted for an easier life but have chosen the way of self-denial and faced enormous risk for the sake of what is right. How frequently we are reluctant to go even so far as risking embarrassment in order to question what is not right.

Haman's problem — or problems!

An illuminating sentence gives us insight into the politics and relationships of the royal court. Verse 4 says: 'Therefore they told Haman about it to see whether Mordecai's behaviour would be tolerated.' The lines of authority need to be tested and interpreted in every social structure and here we have a situation where the royal officials are thinking 'if he can get away with not bowing down, then what other compromises might there be?' Those who were not secure wanted to check out as much as possible which way the wind was blowing, how the rise in status of one affected the pecking order for the rest of them; to find out what it meant if they wanted to disobey Haman over an issue.

Haman was enraged when he heard of Mordecai's stubborn refusal to honour him. He was so pompous and sure of his own importance, he could not cope with his status not being recognised by a mere Jew. The fact that Mordecai was Jewish appeared to touch a raw nerve for Haman. Haman displays a prejudice and discrimination like others; his anti-Semitic and racist attitudes were born out of jealousy at success or fear of difference. If only such prejudice were a thing of the past.

A newspaper article from *The Times*[6] covered the issue of anti-Semitism. The title of the article was '*Paranoid? We have every reason to be*'. One headline stated: 'In this age of political correctness and tolerance Britain thinks it has rid itself of anti-Semitism but love opened Philip Norman's eyes to the truth.' Philip Norman, a non-Jew, married Sue, a Jew, and he explains how over the years they have suffered a range of anti-Semitic comments such as: 'It does make you think that Hitler may have had a point,' said by a friend of the family. Worse than that he wrote of direct verbal attacks in smart London suburbs where at the school gate parents' comments included: 'There are too many ****** Jews around here.' Norman also speaks of a Jewish charity worker finding on his doorstep some old boots and a passport application for Canada. 'Canada' was the block at Auschwitz where guards sorted out the clothes and shoes of the Jewish men, women and children who'd been stripped naked and herded into the gas chamber.

The malice and vindictiveness with which people express their prejudice has an endless sick creativity. Without knowing, or perhaps with full understanding, people cripple and torture others with their hurtful words and actions.

Having learned that Mordecai was Jewish, Haman determined to extract the greatest amount of revenge that he could for this affront to his position. He was determined to punish not just Mordecai but the whole nation of Jews through the whole of Xerxes' kingdom. This reveals Haman in his true colours – more than just a maggot he is a vile apology for a person created in God's image. He is the early role model for the likes of Hitler, Milosevij and Pol Pot. There was no justification for his actions, the punishment far outweighed the original offence. It appeared that Haman had been looking for an opportunity to show his power and to prove to everyone how important he was. To slaughter a whole nation for one person's offence is a terrible evil and injustice – the action of a person whose conscience has been so dulled and so perverted that he has no grasp of right or wrong.

Haman's Achilles' tendon

Haman's real problem was that he was never satisfied. He had status above all the other aristocrats, he had wealth, he had power, he had influence. All the other courtiers bowed down to him except Mordecai – and that left Haman very discontented. He could not enjoy the success he had: he always needed to have more. This lack of contentment was further compounded by pride, a lack of appreciation and gratitude for all he had achieved. Haman was arrogant and demanding with an attitude that expected everything.

Probably one of the saddest aspects of our society is people's lack of contentment. From the multimillionaire who is always looking to make the next million, to the more humble worker who has more than enough, most people strive for more. It is built into all of our economic and business systems that we should want more. Our economic structures depend on more people wanting and consuming more, more of the time. We are targeted by marketing strategies to want things we don't need and to need things we don't want.

Lack of contentment is a real danger for all of us. We cause ourselves all kinds of unnecessary stress. We commit ourselves to higher paid jobs and more demanding work, and life becomes too pressurised to cope with. Recent research has shown that a lot of what we buy we don't really want but just want to have what other people haven't got or to show we've got the same. What seems so exciting and satisfying materially is such a pitiful shadow of the real fulfilment which comes from relationships with God and his people. There is an urgent need for Christians to be content and to enjoy what God has given, not always to be looking for the next material 'fix'. If you want to work towards a more contented life, make a conscious effort to manage without something each week – A meal out, a new CD, a tie or pair of shoes. Live more simply and learn to appreciate what you have. Pray for contentment and seek to avoid the pressure to have more and find fulfilment in things. It is a battle, and the odds are weighted against us in our marketing-mad world. If only we can say with Paul in Philippians 4:12: 'I have learned the secret of being content in any and every situation.' Paul had faced everything– the good life and the most appalling difficulties, but through it all he had learned to know Christ and be content in Him.

Truth, half-truth and lies (3:7-11)

Having determined to annihilate the whole Jewish race Haman set about organising a plan to fulfil his diabolical objectives. Those in the pay of Haman, keen to ingratiate themselves to him, cast the Pur or the lot to decide which day was most propitious to the gods on which to carry out this deed so that they were guaranteed success. This was a common method of guidance, getting a sign by throwing symbols (a little like dice), and seeing which date is revealed. The word Pur becomes significant later as the salvation of the Jews by God through Esther and Mordecai is celebrated in the festival of Purim, which is derived from the word for casting a lot.

The date that was revealed was in the twelfth month, and the time of the casting of the lot was in the first month. Haman had eleven months to organise the genocide. The Jews had eleven months to live in fear and trembling. Everything points to the Jews being treated as worthless. Their feelings were regarded as irrelevant, their future expendable and their lives insignificant. To the Persians the Jews were not real people - they behaved as if they were a subspecies. This is a danger for all of us, of dehumanising those with whom we disagree, of treating them like animals, referring to them as pigs, rats, vermin or snakes. When someone has acted in an underhand, unjust, duplicitous, vile manner it is easy to speak of them as if they are a subhuman species. While the reaction to their activities may justify such language in expressing disgust, the use of subhuman vocabulary demeans the speaker and the subject. We may find it hard to believe but even our worst enemy is created in the image of God and for that reason alone warrants respect as a person not as an animal.

If we refer to people in such a way it becomes a downward spiral of abuse and people draw the conclusion that if they are described in animal terms then they will behave in such a manner. The end result is that people can no longer be rational, no-one takes responsibility for their actions and a poor relationship or open hostility deteriorates even further. Respect in any and every situation is required to avoid a range of long term problems. Festering open wounds from careless comments and unhelpful language can take generations to heal.

Haman needed to report such a significant event to Xerxes and does so whilst being economical with the truth. He does not explain who the people are but focuses on the fact that they are different and that they do not obey the king's laws, which is a misrepresentation. It was Mordecai who was refusing to participate in one aspect of the king's command – not the whole nation that had been disobedient. There is a vague, generalised comment that it is not in the king's best interest to tolerate them – as if he were talking about weeds or some minor irritation, not a race of people.

To sweeten the plan even further, Haman offers Xerxes the equivalent of 340 tons of silver; a huge amount with which to swell the royal treasury, confiscated from the Jews who were to be annihilated. The king politely offers to allow Haman to keep the spoils of his activity which would be consistent with Eastern manners and custom, but they would both know that Xerxes expected the royal coffers to benefit substantially from this massacre and confiscation of goods. The king would turn a blind eye to whatever Haman did and whatever Haman acquired for himself.

King Xerxes, having such confidence in Haman, gave him authority to do as he pleased with these people. Persian kings were easily swayed by their favourites and since Haman portrayed the Jews as traitors it is not surprising that Xerxes followed his plan so willingly. Note the Jews are never named as a race before Xerxes. While people remain anonymous they are somehow not fully human. Once a name and face are added to the picture it is much harder to act with such callous indifference.

There are those who struggle with the historical accuracy of this particular aspect of the book of Esther. It seems unlikely that Haman would have fixed the date so far ahead and that a major annihilation would have been started by one man's defiance. To have such doubts is to portray a naïve ignorance of human nature and the human condition. Wars and massacres have been triggered by the most trivial of incidents often because greater problems and tensions lie underneath, the war or the outcome in no way being justified by the original insult or upset. The injured pride of a powerful person is an unstable, dangerous cocktail – 'Hell hath no fury like a woman scorned.' Similarly, we might comment that hell has no fury like those with status whose fragile ego is offended.

We see in Xerxes an irresponsible fool, someone who was happy for others to make decisions and to have authority in the kingdom as long as he wasn't troubled too much. Xerxes himself may not have been evil but he was culpable because he failed to take full responsibility for the things he should have. He lost touch with what was going on. He was hemmed in by those who fed him a diet of information which was filtered and he only heard what they wanted him to hear. He lived a cocooned life of luxury and wealth, with those around him who would ensure he was not disturbed as long as their personal agendas were followed.

I wonder whether it is so different today. Our leaders, if they are not careful, can become isolated from reality and live in such a busy whirl of meetings, press interviews and political pressure that anyone who offers to off-load some of the burden, whatever their motives, is welcomed with open arms. I remember Lord Owen speaking about the time he was Foreign Secretary and saying that life was so busy, travelling around the world and caught up in a constant programme of meetings, diplomacy and socialising that he had no time to read the newspapers or to have contact with ordinary people. He relied on summaries and main points being extracted for him by others. Everything he received was prepared and filtered for him by others. Fine when the people supporting you are wise, loyal and have integrity; a problem if they are not.

Haman's evil planning continues – it is stomach churning stuff. He was a leader with no moral conscience or consideration, who saw only his own personal interest and regarded other people as totally dispensable in his plans and activities. In 3:13 we read: 'Dispatches were sent by couriers to all the king's provinces with the order to destroy, kill and annihilate all the Jews – young and old, women and little children – on a single day, the thirteenth day of the twelfth month, to plunder their goods.' Sadly such things do not surprise us, we know too much of modern day genocide to be surprised by such inhuman barbarity. The killing fields of Cambodia, Rwanda, Northern Ireland, Kosovo – the list could go on, of the number of places where one group has tried to extinguish another. The twentieth century and no doubt the twenty-first century will have its fair share of Hamans.

Susa reels in shock (3:15)

The king and Haman sat down to drink but the city of Susa was bewildered. Xerxes had been completely duped. He was not aware of what was going on; that he had just signed the death sentence for his own wife. He sat and drank while the citizens of Susa tried to grasp the full significance of the edict that had been proclaimed. He showed himself a fool again, not unlike Nero who fiddled whilst Rome burnt.

The potential for human destructiveness should drive us to our knees. We should be praying for God's protection against such monstrous acts and the indifference of those who have the power to change things. I am reminded of that well-known saying, 'All it takes for evil to triumph is that good men do nothing.' Xerxes may not have been a particularly bad king, although I have my doubts, but Haman was able to do what he wanted because Xerxes surrendered responsibility and abdicated involvement in running the empire.

While Xerxes and Haman drank, the citizens of Susa were bewildered and stunned. They could not believe that the people they lived amongst, worked alongside, laughed and cried with were to come to such an awful end. As in most societies it is likely that the Jewish community had contributed a great deal to the economic and social fabric of Susa. For those who heard the news they must have thought it was a ghastly mistake but no-one would dare to question the all-powerful Haman.

6

Sackcloth and Ashes

Esther chapter 4

I find it difficult to put myself into the shoes of Mordecai and his people when that edict went out. Just imagine, if you can, what it must be like to be told that you and all your people will be wiped out by an act of law in eleven months' time. The shock, unbelief and terror – what emotion would come to the fore? Despair at the lost future, of hopes unrealised and dreams unfulfilled, grandchildren never seen, marriage not achieved, adulthood only aspired to?

The anger and outrage at the injustice and evil, the helplessness and dismay at the hopelessness and impotence. There must have been those who expressed their anger to God. Why? – they must have shouted out loud, with bitterness and despair. Why us again Lord? These are the people who have already seen their land conquered and their people exiled. They have been humiliated and reduced to a remnant as it is. Why this final slaughter? Had their history of rebellion and disobedience led to this?

As we reflect on the Jewish people at this time we look around the world and see so many other people wondering 'why us?' The Tutsi, the Cambodians, the Tamils, Kosovo Albanians, Chechneyans, Serbians, Basques, Gypsies. Groups around the world have faced all kinds of threats to their future and their identity. It is yet more evidence of the fall of humanity; the fact that as God's created people we have moved far from his plan for the way we should live together on this planet. One group constantly tries to have power and control over others. One group is envious or greedy, wanting more land, influence or advantage.

Mordecai and the Jews across the empire responded as would be expected. They wailed and wept, they mourned and fasted and they clothed themselves in sackcloth and ashes. So different to the British stiff upper lip approach. We would try to keep all the emotion in, not show our feelings and pretend we are coping. While recent research suggests it is not always good to give full expression to feelings and that it can help to come to terms with difficulty by having some control of emotions, I do think Eastern cultures have a lot to teach our more restrained Western society. The need to express feelings and not to be inhibited in expressing our pain is all part of the grieving process and I do think if we cut this short, then we find the hurt and repressed feelings find expression in other ways in the long term.

The sackcloth and ashes were a clear symbol of grief and mourning. It would have been clear to all who saw the Jews that they were in despair and that a serious disaster had befallen them.

Ignorance is bliss (4:4-5)

Esther was protected from the political news of the day. Surprising as it might seem, while the rest of Susa knew about the edict and the forthcoming destruction of the Jews, Esther herself was ignorant of all that had happened. She was in an insulated world of royal life, kept distant from matters of state.

In many ways a life of ignorance is a life of bliss. Which reminds me of the school report I frequently wanted to write: 'If ignorance is bliss your son should lead a very happy life.' If only we didn't know about and didn't have to know about so many of the things that go on, life would be a lot easier to cope with. One of the problems with today's instant news coverage of every disaster and human tragedy is that we know too much. It is impossible for us to take in and respond to every situation we hear about, and we have unconscious strategies for coping, either by switching off mentally when we hear about something or not allowing ourselves to reflect too deeply on the issues.

However, as with most things, although we may like to keep distant from painful truth, eventually it has a way of penetrating our protection. Queen

Esther heard about Mordecai in sackcloth and ashes from her maids and eunuchs. She reacted with great distress and was perplexed at what the problem might be, at what had happened to her dependable Mordecai.

It seems that even Esther's attendants were in the dark about what had happened. The king's household was an isolated community unaware of so much that was happening. Immune to the stark realities that faced the rest of Mesopotamia, Hathach, one of her attendants, went to Mordecai to find out the reason for his distress and discovered the awful truth in great detail even down to how much Haman had offered the king.

Mordecai's plea to Esther (4:8)

From all we know of Mordecai so far, it is apparent that he is a person of integrity and wisdom. He is no fool and when he made a request he would be aware of what he was asking. His request to Esther was that she go to the king and plead on behalf of her people. A simple request to us maybe, but to Esther in her role as queen, tied up with all of the court protocol and all of the demands placed upon her, this was no light matter. He was asking her to do the almost impossible, to go to the king and ask for an overturning of the edict when everyone knew how powerful and influential Haman was, and how much he was in the favour of the king.

We have already mentioned that Xerxes had the authority and power of a demigod. He had sanctions over his people that would be an obscenity by modern democratic standards. No-one was permitted to enter the king's presence without being asked by the king. The king did not wish to be troubled by those he did not ask to see. If anyone approached the king without permission then there was just one law – they would be put to death. The only exception to this was if the king held out the golden sceptre to spare their life.

Adding to the problem, as Esther explained in her reply to Mordecai, is the fact that for thirty days she had not been called to the king. This did not bode well for her. She was not a confident mature queen who had the benefit of years of experience – she was young and unsure of herself. She was also alone with her thoughts, unable to discuss in detail what she should do, unable to get the support and insights of those who were like-minded and able to clarify the confusion in her mind. At the time she most needed Mordecai's advice, he was unable to do anything other than direct affairs via others.

Mordecai's reply – a statement of faith (4:12-14)

Esther's attempts at stalling and prevarication cut no ice with Mordecai. The situation is too serious to think about personal safety issues. The matter is one of life and death and life or death risks had to be taken. The chilling response to Esther gave her no comfort, just a greater sense of foreboding. 'Do not think that because you are in the king's house you alone of all the Jews will escape.' Once the killing began and it was discovered that Esther herself was Jewish it is Mordecai's view that it would be difficult for the king to save his wife. The king might feel deceived if she had hidden her origins, and might even think less of her if she had not spoken up on their behalf.

The second part of his reply is a remarkable statement of belief and hope in God. This is the nearest we get to God being mentioned in Esther and while he is not mentioned by name his presence and power is implicit in this statement of Mordecai. 'For if you remain silent at this time, relief and deliverance for the Jews will arise from another place, but you and your father's family will perish. And who knows but that you have come to royal position for such a time as this.' This is a clear statement of God's providence. It is the theological heart of the story of Esther. In a book that does not mention God this is the clearest point at which the implied context of God's controlling and sovereign power breaks through. Providence is a broad concept with a range of nuances and meanings. It is God's care and forethought. It is His continuous activity in upholding creation and all the events of humanity. God fulfils His generous purposes and providence has a clear emphasis on the generosity of God and His gracious provision both in His Creation and in history.

It is the historical aspect of God's providence that is most clearly seen in Esther and is the focus of Mordecai's comment to Esther that if she did not act to save her people then God would deliver His people by another means. Providence in history carries the idea that God has a plan for history. The plan is that since the fall of humankind, God has been acting to bring redemption to all people. Using the Jews as an example to the rest of the human race, God planned to show His character and power. When the nation of Israel rejected God through their neglect of the law and their neglect of true worship, God's plan culminated in Jesus being born as a man and being the redeemer of all.

The Jews have always maintained a special place in God's providence. In a particular way they are His people and His providence is such that He could not allow His people to be annihilated in the way that Haman planned. Mordecai can therefore have confidence because of his knowledge of God whose grace towards his people was such that he would not abandon his people and would act in some way to save his people.

God's providence raises a whole host of

unfathomable questions. It seems incomprehensible that God should allow the evil to do well and let them prosper whereas the godly suffer all manner of disasters. It is difficult to understand why God did not in His providence intervene in disasters where the innocent have suffered, e.g. Aberfan; earthquakes in Italy or San Francisco; floods in Bangladesh. How can we reconcile human freedom with God's providential activity? If God is at work fulfilling His plans through His people, is there any way in which people can be viewed as being free?

An answer is given in that the ungodly only prosper in the short term. Their prosperity is shallow and superficial and will not stand for eternity. The suffering of the godly has been covered in a wide range of writings. C. S. Lewis in *The Problem of Pain*[7] speaks of suffering as: 'God's megaphone to a dying world,' or 'God whispers in our pleasures but shouts at us in our pain.' Suffering, disaster and difficulty are part of life, but they are the part of life that throws us on to God and reminds us of our dependence and reliance on Him.

The question of human freedom is an issue that has to be held in tension. Esther was completely free to choose whether she approached Xerxes or not. If she had chosen not to, God's plans would have continued by another route. God cannot be thwarted and so it is possible to have a doctrine of personal freedom and God's providence. When a person is prompted by the Holy Spirit they have the freedom to follow that leading or to reject it: whatever happens God's will will be fulfilled.

Talk about 'with friends like that who needs enemies'! What a pressure to put on someone else and yet the situation justified the most drastic action. Mordecai spelt out to Esther her options and they were just two and neither of them attractive. She was doomed if she spoke, she was doomed if she was silent. It seemed like the ultimate no win situation. Esther, like many, might have taken the passive role and sought to wait and see, keep her mouth shut and hope the situation was resolved by a miracle. Mordecai makes clear she could do that. Deliverance would come, of that Mordecai had the utmost faith. In that deliverance, she, as the king's wife, may well lose her life and be assassinated along with the king. God would save his people but if she distanced herself from her people at this time then she would ally herself with Xerxes and his court and would face whatever came their way.

Mordecai believed fervently that even in this disaster the sovereign hand of God was at work. There is a redeemer, there is hope. With the eye of faith Mordecai has recognised that it is amazing that Esther is in the exalted position that she is in. He can see the hand of God working out his purposes through her and it seems possible that God has put her in that role for this specific reason. If she failed to meet her responsibilities and the privilege that God had given her, then God would not be thwarted in his plan, but she would not have the delight of sharing in his work.

Esther's place in the palace was not coincidental. She was there at a specific time for a specific purpose. It was an awesome responsibility but the timing was clear. She was in God's schedule. The phrase 'for such a time as this' is a popular saying. It has been used widely in recent years and I am concerned that it has often been applied indiscriminately to all kinds of situations. It has been taken out of its context and used with abandon in a variety of contexts both trivial and significant. There must be some doubt about whether or not this is appropriate. God does place people in different situations for specific purposes of great consequence and yet more are working out God's plan in our routine lives. There is a danger that often we like to think that we are following in the footsteps of Esther when in fact we are claiming too much for ourselves. It is a particular view of guidance. It is often called the blueprint approach. It goes like this: God has a perfect will for us that only we can fulfil and if we fail, then God's plan is undermined and his cosmic purposes are frustrated. It is not a view that I subscribe to. There are exceptional circumstances when God calls us to a specific role but, unlike Esther, we are living in the power of the

Holy Spirit under the new covenant. God's perfect will is more to do with our being rather than our doing. We need a more cautious and circumspect use of the phrase 'for such a time as this'. It is in danger of being so overused that it has lost its value. Yet in other ways each one of us is in a place at a given time for a purpose, to fulfil God's will and that is a helpful reminder to use every opportunity for God's kingdom.

Esther was in Susa in the King's palace for that specific hour to do God's will. It is a foreshadowing of a much more significant hour when Jesus faces the cross. He says, 'Now my heart is troubled, and what shall I say? "Father save me from this hour?" No, it was for this very reason I came to this hour' (John 12:27). It may be that at some point we face an hour in our lives that we would rather God saved us from. It appears to us to be a situation of cosmic proportions that leaves us feeling defeated before we have started and unable to proceed, but God says to us 'this is the reason you have lived, this is the critical point, face it and I will be with you, but face it you must'.

The courage of Esther (4:15-17)

Esther reflected on her dilemma – we don't know too much about timing and how long she spent before answering, but the pace of the narrative gives the impression that no time was wasted. She acted thoughtfully but decisively. She asked Mordecai to gather together all the Jews who were in Susa to fast for her. For three days and nights they were to go without water and food and she and her maids would fast as well. Having taken the time to reflect in God's presence and to hear his wisdom and to show God that she acknowledged her complete dependence on him, she would go in to the king. We are not told that she waited on God and prayed, or that she sought his wisdom and strength, for, as we have said before, God is not mentioned and yet He is so woven into these events. Fasting in the Jewish community would have meant all of these things and Esther determined to maintain her faith and trust, despite the most demanding test she had ever faced.

It is at this point of the story of Esther that she is at her most admirable. This whole chapter portrays her as a woman of humility. She did not presume that the king would listen to her and that her influence would make a difference. As a woman of wisdom, she weighed the options thoughtfully, knowing the potential consequences, not in blissful ignorance of what might happen. She responded willingly but not rashly. She was not foolhardy. Overall she showed enormous courage and a heroic sense of perspective.

Esther was dependent completely on God's overruling and she acted with faith knowing what she hoped would happen, what God could do and yet never presuming to know precisely God's will and purposes. As she faced the coming days she honestly acknowledged the worst that might happen. 'If I perish, I perish.' It would be a greater risk to do nothing. At least she would perish doing what was right – the alternative might be to perish doing nothing. If she did die she would die with a sense that she had acted faithfully to herself, her people and her God.

She was not being dramatic. This was not a heroine of stage and screen with a hand held dramatically to the brow as she exclaims: 'If I die, I die.' This was a woman of integrity who understood the risks, was confident of what was right and was determined to do it. In the safety and security of where you are reading this book it might seem unlikely that you would face the prospect of potential martyrdom and yet there are Christians today in situations where at times they make a decision knowing for them it might mean death - those who take a stand for justice, for truth, for Christian beliefs. Even at the beginning of the twenty-first century they can find themselves threatened with death.

There are many recent examples of those who have faced death for their Christian beliefs. In Uganda in 1977, Bishop Festo Kivengere preached on 'The Preciousness of Life' to an audience including many high government officials. He denounced the arbitrary blood-letting, and accused the government of abusing the authority that God had entrusted to it. The government's response was to arrest Archbishop Janani Luwum, Kivengere's colleague and brother in Christ, ostensibly to search for hidden stores of weapons. The Archbishop called on President Amin to put a stop to the policies of arbitrary killings and the unexplained disappearances of many people. He was not seen alive again.

Archbishop Rameiro from Latin America was systematically persecuted and eventually killed for his fight for justice for the poor. He was remembered for his words when he exclaimed: 'When I feed the hungry I am called a saint, when I seek changes to the injustice that causes hunger, I am called a Communist.'

Alex Muge, the Bishop of Eldorat in Kenya, spoke out against President Moye and he was apparently killed in a car accident that few think of as an accident. Father Popieluszko, a Polish priest, is another example of one who gave his life for the cause of his people. 'Father Jerzy Popieluszko, a popular young parish priest in a suburb of Warsaw, Poland, spoke out against the abuses of communism and supported the then-banned Solidarity labour union. Thousands flocked to hear his Sunday sermons. He was abducted by the Polish secret police on 19 October 1984. His savagely beaten body was found eleven days later in an icy reservoir. Father Popieluszko's death serves as testimony to 'the struggle for freedom, basic rights, and human dignity' (taken from McNichols Icon web-site). Many Christians are facing persecution today in Indonesia, Sudan and other places for their Christian beliefs.

On a lesser level we have said that few of us today find ourselves facing death for our beliefs and actions. That doesn't stop us avoiding risks, remaining silent and keeping a low profile. Mordecai's words can be true for all of us: 'If you remain silent ... deliverance will arise from another place.' And we might add 'but you and your household will miss out on being involved in God's designs and not have the privilege and blessing of knowing that you are in His will.' I rather like Charles Swindoll's way of summing this up: 'Quit protecting your own backside.'[8] What are you really afraid of? Nothing as serious as death for most of us. We are paralysed by our own imaginary fears and uncertainty. We hold on to jobs, reputation and status and risk our rewards in eternity for such paltry things. Take a risk, get a life, follow the example of Esther, challenge some of the things around you that are damaging and destructive. We are so reluctant to make a difference for the sake of Jesus. Why do fear of people and anxiety about unknown consequences inhibit us so much? Take a moment to think about how you could step out in faith, move out of your comfort zone, and take a stand on an issue. Invite neighbours around for dinner and tell them about Jesus, start a home group with non-Church people discussing Christian faith, do something that will stretch you, extend your faith. Don't hold so tightly to all the things that you cannot keep so you lose what will last for ever.

Mordecai follows instructions (4:17)

The tables are turned. The instructor becomes the instructed. He who has taught Esther everything now listens and obeys. He does not try to improve on her instructions or alter her request. In God's kingdom, when His business is being done there is no room for standing on status. There are times when those we have trained and led need to be set free to take the initiative and to make decisions. Mordecai is not interested in who is giving the orders or whether the correct procedures and precedents are being followed. He is concerned that justice is done and that God's work is successful. That should be our aim. Not whether it seems appropriate that the person doing the leading is doing so.

As the story moves into chapter 5 and Esther makes a bold stand, it might appear that human intervention is the pivot which shapes events. It is Esther who decides what to do, Esther who gives instructions to the Jews on how they should act and Esther who leads her people in prayer and fasting. On the surface it could appear that it was Esther who changed the situation. What has really happened at this point of events is that Esther, Mordecai and the others from the Jewish community, admit their weakness and their need. In their fasting and prayer they acknowledged that without God they are helpless—it is this which reverses their fortunes. It is in dependence on God that the turning point is reached. This has far-reaching implications for us as we struggle and fight to be strong when God is saying: 'If only you would admit that you are weak.' The implications for us from history are that we are not to store up all the might and strength that we can but to face the fact that in our weakness is God's strength. It is a reminder not to rely on whatever resources we might hold great store by, such as our qualifications, personality, wealth, or status but to recognise that it is in transparent dependence on God that we know supernatural strength. In recognising our weakness we discover the power and blessing of God.

Philippians 4:13 reinforces this: 'I can do all things through Him who gives me strength.' We can do all things in God's will, provided we rely on Jesus and don't think we can do it ourselves. Whatever you face at the moment, and for you it may be the biggest problem imaginable, then God will give you the strength to cope with it. Another verse which springs to mind is 2 Corinthians 12:9, 'His grace is sufficient for me for His power is made perfect in weakness.' In our weakness we display God's glory, in our weakness God is able to work, in our weakness the Kingdom of God is extended and His plans fulfilled.

There was Esther with all the trappings of power and influence but when it came to an issue that really mattered then she was as weak as the rest of us. She was totally dependent on God's intervention and grace. She could only trust and obey what she knew was the right course of action for her to take.

7

Diplomacy, Tact and Dignity

Esther chapter 5

Esther dressed for the occasion. She was going to see the king so she put on her royal robes and waited in the place where she could be seen and where she faced either a death sentence or the opportunity to plead her cause. She showed respect and honour for the king in his position. She did not treat lightly the office he held and she showed deference to him. She dressed in the manner appropriate to his status and had careful regard for correct protocol. This is not the approach that all Christians would take.

There has always been a strand of Christianity that argues we dress up for no-one. We answer to God alone and he looks at the heart (1 Pet. 3:3-4), not the outward appearance. However, Scripture does present the case that authority is a gift from God (Rom. 13:1-6), otherwise there would be disorder leading to anarchy. This includes those in authority who do not acknowledge God, for the role of king and leader, prime minister or president is an office which should receive our respect and our support in prayer. If the person in that office is not worthy of our esteem then still we give due honour to the office if not to the person. I am not convinced by the approach to those in authority that says: 'They are no better than I am, they are only people and I shall behave and dress as I would anywhere.' It is a half truth made into a whole truth and in so doing becomes an untruth. True, they are just people like the rest of us but the office they hold carries with it certain protocols that we do well to observe if we wish to push forward the claims of Christ. We will not endear ourselves to those in authority if we show a wilful disdain for what is culturally proper and respectful practice. Our message will be lost in the manner by which we seek to deliver it. 'Show proper respect to everyone' (1 Pet. 2:17), reinforces the need to defer to those who may not be honoured in the Kingdom of God but who are nevertheless worthy of respect.

While living in Plymouth an annual lifeboat service took place at Mutley Baptist Church. The Lord Mayor, the Port Admiral and a whole range of uniformed dignitaries processed into the morning service, joined worship, listened to the preaching and left with a trumpet fanfare. There were members of the congregation who found it difficult to stand and honour the dignitaries as they entered the building. It seemed as if we were giving honour to people that was due to God alone. Yet that was not the case. What we were doing was showing good manners and an appropriate respect for the offices that those people held.

On one day of the year, graduation day, in the college where I trained, the faculty and graduating students are attired in formal academic dress. The degrees being conferred are university degrees and the day represents a triumph of God's grace in the lives of many people young and old who have battled their way through courses and training for wider ministry. Many have struggled to find the financial support needed, others have had to overcome a variety of obstacles including being separated from family. The day is a celebration of God's goodness, of human achievement and of future hope of ministry and service in God's kingdom. The formal academic dress, the formal processing alongside the joyful worship and inspirational testimonies and message make the day memorable every year. There are, however, leaving students and the occasional speaker who wish to exempt themselves from the academic dress. To them it speaks of a shallow holding to worldly values and they would want the graduation to have little in the way of formality. As the graduation service is currently carried out it impresses many from the university and student families some of whom have little Christian conviction. They listen to the worship and are inspired by the words because the formal proceedings are carried out with such dignity and propriety. In fact the graduation ceremony is a role model for secular institutions of how to send out their students in a more meaningful way, although of course, other colleges and departments can never emulate the worship and the fellowship of a Christian college.

I shudder when I hear of Christians trying to get their message across to influential people without any consideration for the appropriateness of their approach, dress and attitude. Perhaps Paul's policy should apply when he wrote: 'I have become all things to all men that I might at least save some' (1 Cor. 9:22).

The golden sceptre (4:2)

Whoever wrote the book of Esther not only had a sense of humour but also a desire to underplay the melodramatic. I am sure if I had been writing this part of the events as a record for future generations, I would have done more than just present the simple facts. There is no mention of the tension, of Esther's white drawn face, of the king seeing her there and being surprised at her audacity, of that split second which seemed to last a lifetime before the golden sceptre was raised and before she knew whether or not she would perish or was saved.

There is a charming modesty about the account. We are told simply that the king held out the golden sceptre, Esther approached and touched the tip of the sceptre as a symbol of appreciation that the king was not displeased with her interruption. Xerxes realised that this was a major event, that Esther had not just come to pass the time of day and have a cup of tea. Knowing something serious is on her mind he tries to make it easy for her, to smooth the way for whatever her request might be, he is eager to please her. He offers her anything up to half the kingdom. We don't know what he expected Esther to ask for, but it is unlikely that he had in mind what she did request, a banquet with Haman.

Esther reveals herself as the coolest of operators. She doesn't rush in with her appeal— there is an air of enigma and mystery about her. There is also a modesty. Even though she has been offered up to half the kingdom she does not become over-confident, she remains respectful, submissive and self-effacing. She is not demanding or manipulative of the king. However, this is a game of life and death. She has everything to lose. Her ingenuity, resourcefulness and understanding of people are crucial. She plays her part with the skill of a seasoned politician. She uses cunning and wisdom to achieve her goal.

A game of cat and mouse (5:4-8)
Xerxes must have known that Esther was up to something and is apparently quite happy to play along. Haman is his trusted and loyal second in

command and maybe he hoped that this was going to be an entertaining and surprising diversion, that his new wife had thought of some original way of delighting him. The king agreed willingly and so the three of them gather to share the banquet and the king returned to the question of her petition knowing full well that the banquet alone would not have warranted Esther taking such a risk.

Being thoroughly respectful, at Mutley Baptist Churchat Mutley Baptist Church Esther uses delaying tactics again and requests that Haman and Xerxes join her the next day for a second banquet when she promises that she will answer the king's question.

It seems like a cat and mouse game, except Esther is the mouse playing games with the cats. She has fasted, prayed and prepared for this petition to be made and so we know she was seeking to follow God's leading. She was patient, she didn't rush, she waited for exactly the right time, for God's moment of success. Most of us are much too impatient as far as God's timing is concerned. We live in such an instant society, where everything happens immediately and people are encouraged to wait for nothing, that spiritually we can find it difficult to follow God's plans. He knows the pace at which things can be handled and dealt with. We only see from a narrow perspective, certainly not the perspective of eternity.

It is not until Esther has delayed three times that

she makes her final request which is a little perplexing. Why wait for the third opportunity before making clear her petition? D. N. Freedman, however, notes the effect of her delay. She makes her request only when Xerxes has asked three times what it was she wanted.

'The third time is the charm in literary accounts. It is like the acrobat or magician who deliberately fails twice in trying to perform his most difficult feat, before succeeding on the third try. This enhances the suspense and the expectation of the audience, as well as winning for the performance the applause he deserves but is not likely to get if the audience thinks that there is no danger or limited need of skill to succeed.'[9]

A sad picture of a man
with no future (5:9-14)

Events move on and Haman shows gullible glee at the apparently successful developments, but his positive frame of mind was short lived. One of the saddest kinds of people is those who have everything and enjoy nothing. Those who have everything to be happy about and yet have an insatiable appetite for more and an unconquering sense of dissatisfaction. Haman becomes a tragic comic figure. He is misjudging, not understanding, handling situations with an indifference to all the signals that are sent out. Combine that in your thinking with Haman as a Mohammed Ali type figure, proclaiming: 'I am the greatest'. No humility, only an awareness of all that he has accomplished and all that he has gained.

Haman was excited and in high spirits. He had been invited to dine with the king and queen, the only person to share a banquet with them. He thought he had reached the social and political top, but this proved and reinforced his own sense of self-importance. All the things that he valued, all that his ambitious nature hoped for, was coming to pass. He was happy and seemed to lead a charmed existence. He didn't smell a rat even though the invitation to two banquets must have seemed slightly odd. He was too blinded by his own ego to notice what was really going on. As an Agagite he would not have been familiar with the Jewish scriptures, otherwise he might have taken warning from the many Proverbs that speak of the danger of pride and boasting. 'Pride goes before destruction, a haughty spirit before a fall' (Prov. 16:18). Haman was falling into one of the most obvious and destructive of traps, opening himself to the biggest day of reckoning he could imagine.

His ecstatic frame of mind was quickly shattered. It lasted for a brief moment, until journeying through the king's gate, he saw Mordecai, which makes me wonder whether Haman suffered from some kind of manic condition. To go from such heights to such depths emotionally in a short time might indicate an imbalance or lack of stability. I often think that to scale the heights politically requires such a single-mindedness and a determination that it encourages certain personality types that are not always fitted to that office. To achieve high office you need to be slightly unbalanced; to be successful in office you need to be a stable and secure personality. Few can achieve high office and be successful there.

The fly in the ointment

Mordecai, sitting in his usual place by the king's gate, showed neither respect nor fear, which filled Haman with a wrath and a venom that almost heats the page as we read it. We might have thought that Haman in such a positive frame of mind could have ignored Mordecai and not allowed his moment of greatest glory to be spoilt by such a person. All that Haman had achieved, all that had been gained is nothing to him whilst Mordecai still exists. There is a pattern in the lack of contentment of those who prosper by evil intent. Prosperity gained by honest toil is satisfying and pleasurable. Prosperity gained by other methods can bring a whole range of uncomfortable pressure with it. It is difficult to sit back and enjoy the pleasure of success if there is guilt about how the success was achieved or worry about being found out.

Haman constructs his
own punishment (5:10-14)

Interestingly we are told that Haman managed to restrain himself despite being filled with rage at Mordecai's continued insubordination. When he arrives home he shares the news of his good fortune. He brags, he boasts, he gloats and crows. He lists in detail his wealth, his sons (significantly in that order), the honour that the king has given him and the high office he inhabits and finally he announces he has been invited to a banquet with Queen Esther. I am amazed he has any friends at all. Someone who spends their time gloating is not usually the best company, but then the rich and famous never have trouble finding friends of sorts.

Having rattled off his list of accomplishments, Haman acknowledges the dissatisfaction he feels because of Mordecai. Haman's friends agree with him and probably encourage him. They confirm he deserves respect—even more so now that he is on personal speaking terms with the queen, that is the equivalent to being family. Mordecai must be punished for his disrespect and people must be made to see that Haman is too important to be treated in such a way. Haman's so-called friends together with his wife suggest that a gallows should be built, to hang Mordecai on. This was not to be an ordinary gallows but a set of gallows three times the normal height to prove a point that anyone who did not show due respect would be strung up high as an example to all. Haman was taken by this idea. He was too self-seeking and gullible, too absorbed in himself, to see the danger of what he was doing.

There is a reminder in this part of the events of Esther that we should choose our friends with care, particularly if we are in leadership. Be careful when you receive compliments from friends. Are they speaking the truth or what you want to hear? Are they trying to ingratiate themselves or are they speaking with integrity? Those closest to us and those who love us will sometimes say what we want to hear or will often interpret circumstances from a similar perspective, with the same viewpoints in mind. When you want to understand what is going on around you, when you need guidance or have an important decision to make and you need advice, have the confidence to ask people whose comments won't be tainted by self-interest, loyalty or an unwillingness to disappoint. It would save a lot of frustration if we had the courage to seek really objective advice and attempted to stand back from situations rather than be carried away by what we want to be happening.

8

The Silent Hand of God

Esther chapter 6

The silent hand of God (6:1-4)

So far we have seen a compelling story of intrigue, threatened ethnic cleansing, good and evil poised against each other and evil in the person of Haman - seeming to hold all the trump cards. How will it all end? The pace changes abruptly at this point and we leave the busy construction of a huge gallows to the quiet and peace of the king's bedchamber. The whole of the story of Esther seems to turn on a bout of insomnia. The king couldn't sleep, a minor thing in itself but with major consequences. The king was restless and irritated so he asked for the recent records of his reign. Quite a reasonable act but it was the first nail in the coffin of Haman and a subtle sign of God moving to fulfil His purposes.

I wonder how often we fail to perceive God changing events by the most minor occurrences in someone's life. God uses the strangest developments for his glory and to protect his people. So when Xerxes couldn't sleep he read the book of the chronicles (not the Biblical book of that name but the official record of all that happened during his reign), and he was reminded of Mordecai and his part in protecting the king from the conspiracy of Bigthana and Teresh (Esth. 2:21-23).

In being reminded of Mordecai's loyalty and protection the king was aware that a serious omission had occurred because Mordecai had not been honoured. Xerxes was determined to right that wrong and so we build up with almost pantomime humour to the utter humiliation and mortification of Haman.

God's humour and the beginning of Haman's downfall (6:4-14)

The pantomime gets into full swing in this section. The only person in court at that time was Haman, who was intent on getting the king's permission to do full justice, or injustice, to Mordecai. The audience knows what the king is thinking, but Haman does not. There is a glorious buildup as Haman sets himself up for a bigger and bigger fall. Being so proud and conceited, vain and arrogant, when the king asked Haman how he could honour someone Haman presumes it is him. I have a suspicion that Xerxes is playing along with Haman. Although he values him as a second in command and enjoys off-loading responsibility on him he probably recognises his weaknesses and plays on them without realising the terrible scenario he is setting up. There is a kind of double misunderstanding: the king not knowing how Haman feels about Mordecai, Haman not knowing how the king feels about Mordecai. It is a mix up and a farce worthy of many a comedy writer.

Not knowing it is Mordecai to be honoured, Haman thinks of the most extravagant and pretentious methods of honouring a person. His pride leads him to show no reserve in the suggestions that he makes; the things that his inflated ego craved – the shallow material benefits of fame and power. His requests are as close to claiming kingship as they could possibly be – a robe that the king himself has worn, a horse that the king has ridden, with a royal crest on its head. The honoured man is then to be led around the streets of the city by one of the most noble princes, to the acclaim of all the people.

Let us learn from Haman because pride is a dangerous thing. It makes us think we are better than others, more important than others and can blind us to our dependence on God. Pride is what leads to all kinds of other failings. It is the original sin and it shows itself in all kinds of ways. We think we should have more than others and so we get greedy. We think that we should have more recognition and so we fail to give God the glory. Pride is taking from God the glory he deserves and claiming it for ourselves. It is not being able to admit our mistakes and having to cover them up and then being found out later.

Let me be personal for a moment

• Are you proud of the way you look? You may be beautiful, handsome, slender, fit and athletic, with huge eyes and fine bone structure. Be thankful for that but don't be proud. How can you take credit for something over which you had no control, that is a matter of genes and God's graciousness to you.

• Do you have a great gift or talent? Do you have a brilliant degree, are you an astonishing musician, a great sports person, a superb intellect? God has given you those gifts and abilities–be thankful but remember they don't make you better than anyone else, more deserving than anyone else, there is no room for pride.

• Are you wealthy or powerful, influential or famous – don't be proud. It will give you a false sense of importance and an inability to appreciate your relationship to your heavenly Father and probably an inability to see yourself clearly in relation to others.

• Is your house cleaner, neater and tidier than your neighbours? A cause of pride for some. Are your cakes a little lighter and tastier than everyone else's? Is your DIY more impressive?

C. S. Lewis in his book *Mere Christianity*[10] writes of pride being the essential vice and the utmost evil, leading to every other vice: 'it is the complete anti-God state of mind.' He goes on to say: 'Pride gets no pleasure out of having something, only out of having more of it than the next man. We say that people are proud of being rich, or clever, or good-looking, but they are not. They are proud of being richer, or cleverer, or better-looking than others. If everyone else became equally rich, or clever, or good-looking there would be nothing to be proud about. It is the comparison that makes you proud: the pleasure of being above the rest. Once the element of competition has gone, pride has gone. That is why I say that pride is essentially competitive in a way that other vices are not.'

Pride is never far from the surface for any of us. For all of us it is destructive and damaging. Most of us who are proud are too proud to see it. We look down on others and don't realise that we are doing it and fall into the gravest trap. We do not see ourselves as God sees us.

Haman is a warning to us to avoid the sin of presumption which follows pride. He presumes the king wants to honour him, he presumes he can punish Mordecai without permission, he presumes that because he has achieved great wealth and status, he can do just what he wants. Presumption is an arrogance which leads to an emotional blindness, not being able to read situations correctly or relate sensitively to others. It is a trap for the unsuspecting that – like Haman – can lead to all kinds of follies at best and a serious downfall at worst.

Once Haman has suggested honour fit for a king, Xerxes agrees with his recommendations. 'Do it all.' How excited Haman must have been, imagining himself on that horse with everyone applauding and honouring him. No returning FA cup winners, neither Arsenal nor Manchester United, would receive such adulation. He would be talked about across the whole empire, never would there have been such acclaim given to someone like him. He had probably, in his mind, married his children to the king's future offspring and seen himself in the most exalted company. His dreams were short lived. 'Do not neglect anything you have recommended,' said Xerxes, 'do just as you have suggested for Mordecai the Jew.' His jaw must have dropped the furthest in history. His face must have fallen like an avalanche. His avowed enemy, the one he was going to hang, the one who was causing him so much anger and dissatisfaction - this was the one the king wished to honour.

Haman's humiliation was half complete as God's humour sparkles through. Haman who had been so foolish, so empty-headed, in his pride has to honour his enemy. Haman had to lead Mordecai through the streets of Susa while everyone revered him. As an Agagite who believed in chance Haman must have realised that his luck had just left him, that somehow things were not going as he planned, that the signs were not promising. The castles in the sky Haman had been building crashed around him as he realised that he had completely misjudged the situation. Haman is perhaps beginning to realise that he is not the greatest.

Mordecai himself must have been mortified by events. From what we have learnt of him so far, the last thing he would have wanted was to be paraded around on a royal horse and in royal robes. There was no pleasure in that when his people were to be slain. He suffered the praise with no enjoyment and when the parade was over he returned to the king's gate. He had no false sense of self-importance, nor had he any desire to capitalise on the superficial status he had been given. In humility and trust was the way ahead for him, the complete opposite to Haman.

Going home to his wife and friends Haman was covered in grief. Thinking himself so powerful and having such clear plans of what he was going to do, he found himself desolate, despondent and in despair. His friends and family had only a short time to advise him. They wisely suggested that he could not stand against Mordecai now he had been honoured so publicly by the king and he seemed to be so popular. The people of Susa must have been confused. One day their king is passing out edicts to slaughter all the Jews and then not much later the king is giving the highest honour to a Jew. They surely must have wondered what was happening.

Who was in control? Was anyone in control or were they just at the mercy of capricious political moods? Not so much different from today!

One final thought before moving on to further events. So far, in what has happened, there have been a number of coincidences. Haman entered the court as Xerxes was reading the records of his reign and wondering how to reward Mordecai. Before that Xerxes couldn't sleep and happened to read and be reminded of Mordecai and his loyal service. Prior to that Mordecai was in the right place to overhear the plot and to be able to make the king aware of the threat there was on his life. The whole catalogue of apparent coincidences are really insights into God moving. On their own, these don't seem significant. But there is a pattern and it does seem that the life of faith is a catalyst for divine coincidences, supporting our faith and reminding us that God never does leave us or forsake us.

Don't take coincidences for granted. Look to see the pattern that is unfolding and the story that God is weaving in your life. I wonder how often we miss what God has done and is doing because we lack the insight and the understanding of his way of moving in the routine affairs of life, injecting his direction and perspective.

9

Hoisted on his own petard

Esther chapter 7

Haman has started down the slippery slope of his downfall. In chapter 7 his descent becomes so rapid that he careers out of control unable to stop himself falling into his own trap.

The vivid telling of the events of Esther's second banquet with Xerxes and Haman records for us dramatic affairs and the astonishing moving of God's hand in politics and matters of state. The king asks again what the queen's petition is, offering once more up to half the kingdom. At last Queen Esther gives her reply, maintaining her modest and unassuming manner. She presumes nothing and asks with great respect and dignity, she argues her case carefully and thoughtfully. She makes it clear that this is a matter of the gravest concern.

She must have shocked Xerxes when she asked that her life be spared. This would have been the first that Xerxes knew of her life being under threat. She is brave – she does not pretend to be other than Jewish and she only asks for her people to be saved after having first put herself fully in the firing line. She could have shaped her argument in such a way that she tried not to identify herself with the annihilation that faced her people but she did not. She maintains her respect for Xerxes by reinforcing that she would not have bothered him unless it was a matter of life and death. If her people had been sold into slavery she would not have counted that worthy of disturbing the king. Indeed, in some respects her people were already in a kind of slavery since they were in exile.

With her carefully crafted argument she got from Xerxes exactly the response she required. 'Who is he? Where is the man who has dared to do such a thing?' bellows the king. 'The adversary and enemy is the vile Haman,' replies Esther.

Understandably Haman is terrified: just the day before, he was boasting of his great endeavours, he was gloating about his success, and now he must fight for his skin. His lack of judgement and his misunderstanding were as great as they could possibly be and he needed to do all he could to limit the price he would have to pay for his folly and arrogance.

The king, speechless it appears with anger and rage, left his wine and went out into the palace garden to reflect on what he should do next. He may have known that Haman had his weaknesses but to be so totally betrayed and deceived by the one in whom he had put so much trust and to whom he had given so much responsibility, was a disappointment and he felt hugely let down. Further than that, he may have been angry at his own lack of wisdom in appointing Haman to such high office and allowing him to get so far in fulfilling such a calamitous plan.

Anyone in leadership will want to be able to delegate, and part of training up a new generation of leaders is to give responsibility to others and to take risks at times. Often the risk is worthwhile and the leader is rewarded with the companionship of a person of experience, judgement and energy. When the decision to delegate or to hand over responsibility fails, there is a sense of being let down and other emotions enter, such as self-doubt, as questions are asked about the leader's judgement and wisdom. We cannot expect to get leadership issues right all of the time. It is part of our pilgrimage to face disappointment in people when they neglect their duty or fail in their role, but the pain of situations and the hurt caused cannot be avoided.

Haman lacked judgement in many ways but not on this occasion. He knew he was in the deepest trouble possible and he knew nothing was beneath him at this desperate stage of events. Knowing it was almost certain that the king would punish him with death, as the king retreated to the garden, Haman stayed with Esther to beg for his life. In an unfortunate, clumsy act, Haman compounds his problems –as if they weren't dire enough already.

He fell on the couch beside Esther. This was highly inappropriate behaviour. First, she was the queen and secondly, this was a society where women were not approached by any other than their family members. For Haman to place himself in close proximity to the queen where she was reclining was an act of great presumption and gross ill manners. The immediate interpretation of his behaviour was that he was trying to molest Esther, the queen, while she was in the royal palace.

In the perfect timing that seems to dominate all the occurrences of this book, the king returned from the palace garden and witnessed Haman's indecent, if for the first time, innocent behaviour.

The palace guards, or the royal bodyguards, were alert to the tone and inference in the king's voice and did not need a royal command to know what to do. Maybe Xerxes had summoned them while he was in the garden: whatever the case, they acted without hesitation, seizing Haman in order to avoid any further insult to the king. Haman's face was covered and he was whisked away so that neither the king nor queen should be distressed by his presence longer than was necessary.

Haman's crash from glory continued. One of the eunuchs who attended the king informed Xerxes of the gallows that Haman had constructed on which to hang Mordecai. It was a fitting end for Haman to be hung on his own gallows –so high that everyone could see his evil folly. When Xerxes realised that justice would be done, and that the threat to his wife was over, his fury subsided. He could relax again.

The fall of Haman should give us no pleasure although many of us would naturally take delight in the corrupt and vile being so justly dealt with. There is humour in the way the story of Haman is written, he sets himself up for such a huge fall, and there is a comic sense in which we laugh at the way he is punished with the punishment he intended for the innocent. And yet there are no winners in this situation. The pain and distrust that has been sown by the actions of Haman take more than just the hanging of one man to overcome. Haman's own family and friends have much to fear and have been led into all kinds of corrupt and damaging opinions and thoughts. The threat to the nation of the Jews has undermined confidence and esteem and leaves a people less secure and an empire weaker than it was, because the loyalty and unity have been undermined.

It is easy to see how people would get excited about the death of a corrupt and evil leader. There are many across the world who might be candidates for such punishment if we were making a list. However, our overriding thoughts should not be how pleased we are that an evil monster has been destroyed, but rather we should be distraught at the damage and pain that has been caused by this person. Rarely will the death or destruction of one person be the end of the pain and hurt; the scars remain, and the healing can take generations.

I think particularly of the fall of President Ceausescu of Romania a few years ago now in 1989. I remember seeing the desperate attempt at escape, the TV footage of a trial and then the report of his death by firing squad. Having visited Romania while he was in power and seen the oppression and sadness of a beautiful country– of Christians harassed and persecuted because of one man's abuse of power, I was surprised that there was no pleasure in seeing such a person come to a deserved end. There was an enormous sadness at the wasted years, the trampled lives, the missed generation. To have taken pleasure in such an execution would have been to have fallen into the trap of Haman–to have gloated over someone else's misfortune and to have been in danger of thinking that we are better than we really are.

It's not only political leaders who succumb to a weakness of one kind or another. Christian leaders also fail. Those we respect and honour, those who have power and authority in the Church do not always live up to the unrealistic expectations that we have of them. Some fall very publicly. Their humiliation is well-known and their reputation is left in tatters. It is not helpful for anyone to be pleased at this or to gain a sense of satisfaction. It is a sadness that it has happened. Whatever the justice we might see in the final outcome, our response should be of wanting to bring restitution and healing. A response of triumph or gloating will only put us in danger of falling ourselves.

10

It's not over 'til it's over

Chapter 8

You might wonder – having had the happy ending – why there are another three chapters of Esther. All that is significant seems to have happened. But how misleading that is. So often we think the final curtain falls and it's all over but those who are involved know with any event the final curtain is only the concluding of the public aspects of things. Working out all the detail, clearing up all the debris, sorting things out takes time and can sometimes be more demanding than the event itself.

A victory may have been won, and an enemy vanquished, but dealing with the fall-out, coping with the loose ends and confusion, ensuring that the victory is secure and that all the necessary consequences are achieved take time, energy and courage – sometimes more than winning the initial struggle. So many in Christian ministry have been involved in activities where a great success has been achieved, and good things have happened but still there is a lot to be done. Just when you might relax a little, be off your guard and think things don't matter is the very time when all that has been won could, in an unguarded moment, be lost.

Xerxes opens his eyes (8:1-10)

Xerxes must have wondered how he could have missed so much of what was going on. Haman, whom he thought was a loyal leader and commander, turned out to be a traitor. He knew Mordecai was a Jew, but he must have been amazed to discover that he was related to his wife and that she too was a Jew. On discovering all of this and all that his wife had been through at the hands of Haman, the king gave Esther all of Haman's estate as compensation.

Mordecai was introduced to Xerxes as a relative of Esther, and Xerxes, having claimed back his signet ring from Haman, presented it to Mordecai. Xerxes began to understand who his real friends were. Esther appointed Mordecai to be manager of her newly acquired estate knowing whom she could really trust.

At this stage Xerxes still had not given Esther an answer to her original plea. She had made her request that her people should be saved but, overtaken by other events, Xerxes had not said whether or not he would overturn the plans and edicts instigated by Haman. However, it has to be said, things were looking hopeful.

I am astounded by Esther's continued lack of presumption and apparent modesty in all situations. Xerxes has awarded her with Haman's estate but still she is not confident in her original request. She continues to show the utmost respect and honour for her husband. Verse 3 tells us that, 'she pleaded with the king, falling at his feet and weeping. She begged him to put an end to the evil plan of Haman the Agagite.' Again the king extended the golden sceptre to her and she was able to expand on her request without fear of harm. She outlined precisely to Xerxes the sentence that hung over her people. Her advocacy of her people's cause has a happy outcome. Xerxes instructs Mordecai to use the signet ring he has so recently been given to good effect. Mordecai is to write another decree stating whatever is necessary to protect the Jews from the plans of Haman. Once sealed by the king's signet it could not be revoked.

Acting without delay, Mordecai summoned all the royal secretaries and they wrote out orders to everyone with power in the empire. The satraps (the title of a provincial governor in ancient Persia – under Darius I, the Persian Empire was divided between some 20 satraps, each owing allegiance only to the king. Later the term was used to describe any local ruler, often in a derogatory way), governors and nobles of all 127 provinces were informed, each in the script of their province so there could be no mistaking the change of plan. The fastest and best horses were used to speed the message to the farthest reaches of the empire in the shortest possible time.

The protection afforded the Jews (8:11-13)

The edict was strongly worded, offering the Jews the ultimate in protection and rights of defence. The Jews were given the king's authority to assemble and protect themselves and to even kill anyone who threatened them, whatever province or military background they had. Any who might attack or threaten their children and women or plunder their possessions had no rights against the Jews. On a particular day the Jews were given the right to avenge themselves. From being a powerless minority in a foreign land they had become a people with special rights and particular privileges in the empire.

**The mighty have fallen the
humble are raised (8:15-17)**

To see good triumphing and evil vanquished gives a sense of satisfaction and pleasure. Justice being seen to be done is a source of some gratification. That is the picture given to us in these final verses of chapter eight. Haman has been punished and buried and Mordecai has been transformed.

Just a few days earlier Mordecai was in sackcloth and ashes. Now he suddenly found himself dressed in royal robes, wearing a crown and acclaimed with celebrity status across Susa. He must have been pinching himself at the rapid change of circumstances.

'For the Jews it was a time of happiness and joy, gladness and honour ... with feasting and celebrating.' The story of Esther opened with a feast and banquet and at the close there is also feasting and celebration. The second celebration is not a matter of indulgence, pride or boasting but a genuine and sincere rejoicing in having been saved from mass slaughter.

Those of us brought up in the more formal sections of the church family are hesitant to celebrate too much. 'Everything in moderation', is a phrase that springs to mind as one I have heard frequently when limits and constraints are imposed. It is argued that we must not waste God's provision and we must be good stewards of his resources—both laudable views. However, there is so much in scripture of God's abundant grace, of a God when he could just provide a few litres of wine provides enough to almost swim in (John 2:1-11). When he fed the 5,000 not only was there enough for everyone but masses left over to feed thousands more (Mark 6:30-44). It is fitting at times that our response to Him, not only in worship but in all our celebrations of his goodness, is an extravagant gesture reflecting our thanks and gratefulness. A measured response is a meagre action to such a generous God.

A curious note (8:17)

The transformation of the Jews' fortunes is complete. From being the oppressed they have become the victors, from being the powerless they have gained sanctions and support which are a political miracle. Such a turn around in their prospects is astonishing. The almost vanquished become the victors, a definite case of 'he who laughs last, laughs loudest'.

So great is their change of circumstances that many others sought to join them. 'Many people of other nationalities became Jews because fear of the Jews had seized them.' Another insight into human behaviour is given to us in this closing verse. It is a portrayal of a timeless scene that could be taken from any century. People change sides as a matter of expediency.

People like to be on the winning side and often loyalty loses out to other self-interests. When the Jews were down they lost friends and supporters because people did not want to be associated with them as they feared for their own safety. Once the Jews were in a powerful position those around them changed allegiance as a matter of convenience. Many became Jews as a matter of expediency not as a matter of conviction. Human nature does not change down the centuries. There are many today whose loyalty and allegiance is shallow, who will happily change their commitment and devotion according to who offers the best deal, the most security, the least threat.

It is astonishing in the area in which I live the number of people who become Church of England members when their children are getting near to secondary school age, so they can get them into the Church of England secondary school. Others might pretend allegiance to other organisations for pecuniary gain. This should not happen in the Christian Church. The Gospel demands should make it plain that what is to be gained is not necessarily of benefit in this life and won't automatically give us a step up the social or career ladder. Our motives can be extremely warped and muddled as can those of others. We should not go to a particular church because it has better social standing but because it is where God wants us to be. We should be loyal to our Lord and his leading in our lives whether it takes us along smooth and comfortable paths or bumpy and difficult ways. Our commitment should not be a matter of being a fair-weather follower, but a disciple of Christ in all seasons.

11

Triumphant Jews

Chapter 9

Triumphant Jews (9:1-4)

The thirteenth day of the twelfth month, the month of Adar, the day the edict of Xerxes was carried out, was a day of triumph for the Jews. Although the original threat to the Jews had come from just one man, Haman, it is evident from the opening verses of this chapter that the Jews had many enemies. Many relished the prospect of the Jewish downfall and they had hoped to have the upper hand to settle many grievances and benefit from looted property and acquiring land from Jewish owners.

When we think of anti-Semitism our minds often go to the Holocaust, to the slaughter of six million Jews in Nazi Germany in the 1940's. Yet anti-Semitism is nothing new. It is not only the Holocaust years when the Jews have been discriminated against, persecuted and abused because of their nationality. Prior to Esther's time, and in every generation since, the Jews have been the subject of discrimination and prejudice.

There are many reasons for prejudice and discrimination – ignorance of someone who is different, fear of losing one's own identity, a desire to have power over others, a concern for personal culture and values, feeling threatened, misunderstandings about varying lifestyles and an arrogance that tries to make one race appear superior to others. However, it seems with the Jews that while all of these things may be relevant there is the additional, if not overriding, factor of them being the people of God. They have held tenaciously to their faith when other Semitic tribes have lost their identity in the passing of history and have simply been absorbed into wider national groups. The Jews are often a successful and disciplined community which leads to jealousy and envy. It seems for reasons that are not their fault they have made enemies and been victimised down the centuries.

In the Christian family there is no place for discrimination or racism of any kind. We need to be alert to the ways in which the subtle tentacles of prejudice pervade our attitudes and behaviour. There is a need to be alert to our own thought patterns and attitudes and we should reflect on the way we relate to and view others. The Church down the centuries has been guilty of the most hideous racism and abuse of others. The Apartheid system of South Africa was supported theologically and argued to be a valid system for a Christian society by many. We would agree that we are all equal in

Christ (Gal. 3:28), but in practice some are more equal than others.

There is a huge challenge to the Church to show the world a harmony and a unity that comes from Christ. In every country there is racism and prejudice of some kind. Some time ago we stayed in Michigan, in a small town which in many ways was idyllic with a Dutch Reformed background where strong Christian values pervaded all that went on. In one corner of town, in poor housing and not reflecting the success of the rest of the community, were those of Hispanic origin. They were treated differently to all the other people in that town. In any society there will be those who because of their origins come at the bottom of the social pile. This is not the Gospel, this is not God's plan for his people. Jesus went to the poor and the marginalised, loved them and gave them a self-esteem that others denied them. A pattern that the Church should follow.

It is not easy for us to put ourselves in the shoes of the Jews in the city of Susa and the rest of the Persian Empire at this time. To understand fully I think we would have needed to have a death sentence taken from us, to have had a lost future restored, to have had mourning and despair changed to relief and freedom, to have been utterly impotent with no control over the present or the future and to suddenly discover there is a strength and power we never dreamed of. They are the people with hope, with a future, with prospects and confidence. The transformation is astounding.

Mordecai had become a figure of considerable influence and power. His reputation spread far and wide so he was known and feared by all. His prominence in the palace was evident as he grew in power.

Revenge is sweet or is it? (9:5-17)
The Jews, having gained so much power and having the upper hand, at last extract revenge on their enemies. These verses are gruesome to read, particularly for those of us who have never lived through a war and have been fortunate enough not to experience violence at first hand. The Jews struck down and killed their enemies, and meted out retribution on those who hated them.

We might be shocked by the apparent sanctioning of revenge when of course Jesus' teaching is to 'turn the other cheek', and 'go the second mile' (Matt. 5:38-42) but we need to remember a number of things.

Firstly, this is a completely different cultural context to today and the Jews followed the teaching of the Torah (the first five books of the Old Testament) and did not have the benefit of the new covenant teaching from Jesus.

Secondly, this was a different age where

defending oneself and one's property could involve violence. Justice was meted out in a much more direct manner than we are used to today. These were the days of 'An eye for an eye and a tooth for a tooth' (Deut. 19:21).

Thirdly, the revenge was carefully controlled. The Jews did not take full advantage of their privileged position and their change of fortune. They did not rampage throughout the empire in a wanton spree of destruction. They took no plunder from any they killed. This is contrary to almost any other war or battle that occurs: in almost all armed combat the unwritten rule is that the spoils of war go to the victor. The victorious side takes whatever they can from those they have defeated. The Jews stand out as different and show that they are not a people who wish to annihilate their enemies but to have the opportunity to protect their own interests and not to gain unfair advantage over others.

Fourthly, there was no personal benefit from their enemies' demise. They were disciplined and had a sense of purpose in what they were doing. It would have been so easy to justify themselves taking some of the goods and possessions from those they killed, but that would have been to demean themselves and not to show themselves as people set apart from the common culture. Haman was going to take the goods and possessions of the Jews if he had his way, but the Jews were to show that they were different and stood by a different moral code. The backlash of such actions would have been much greater.

In the recent Kosovo conflict the ethnic Albanian refugees returning to Kosovo showed little control in their revenge. Daily, the Serbians faced the revenge attacks of the ethnic Albanians. Homes and shops have been looted, houses and buildings burned. Innocent people are caught up in a nightmare from which the communities may never recover. The damage to relationships, to groups of people who have lived happily side by side is immeasurable. The act of revenge is destructive and often more destructive than the original offence.

Fifthly, the Jews did not give in to the temptation to go too far. It would have been easy to go over the top with their revenge. They had been threatened with the loss of everything. They had been treated as if they were less than the cattle. They had been despised and humiliated. Yet in exacting revenge there was a justice and an ability to do no more than was necessary.

There will be those who still say that the Jews should not have exacted any revenge and should not have killed anyone. That was not an option– it would not have been possible. A severe injustice had been done, the nation had been threatened and punishment had to take place. It would be like suggesting today that a mass murderer is found guilty but the Christian thing to do is to forgive him and not punish him. While we may be able to forgive, the justice of the law must prevail and that is what happened in the situation with the Jews in Susa and the wider empire. For all that the Jews had suffered – the oppression and threats – a just punishment was required.

We also need to get a sense of perspective. Up to 100,000 enemies of the Jews were killed in the Jewish assault on their enemies but six million were killed in the Holocaust. In a world of much smaller populations as it was in Esther's time, it is likely that by comparison the offence was much greater.

What cannot be so easily explained is the increasing number of people today who feel it is their right to exact revenge on others who have offended them. The 'Don't get mad, get even' approach is in common usage and generally supported. In 1998, Anita Liberty made her fortune out of a book entitled '*How to heal the hurt by hating*'. Her boyfriend had finished their relationship and she felt hurt and pained by the manner their relationship ended. She spent the next few months getting revenge. She committed herself to humiliating him in public with as many different embarrassing and demeaning incidents as possible. She described the process as cathartic.

A group of students at a North London University set up the 'Get Back' Agency as part of their Marketing coursework. The purpose of the agency was to offer clients a service for getting revenge, on their behalf, on those who had irritated, offended or hurt them. They set up a spoof agency which they advertised and promoted and included a telephone line to evaluate the success of their promotional techniques. The students were astonished when they received 300 enquiries from the public wishing to use their services.

When we are the victims of unjust situations it is easy to want revenge. If you have been deeply hurt by someone or by events there can be a real desire for getting even, getting one's own back, settling old scores and squaring the account. That means we behave no better than those who have caused the problem to begin with. If it is a legal matter then the judgement of the courts should be enough. If it is not a legal matter or the law lets us down then we need to receive God's grace not to take the matter into our own hands. We are God's people, and can afford to be gracious and forgiving since we know that we are on the winning side. We should also remember Paul's words: 'Do not take revenge, my friends, but leave room for God's wrath, for it is written, "It is mine to avenge; I will repay"' (Rom. 12:19).

The one blot on the moral landscape (9:13)
Esther's request for an extra day in order to

complete the vanquishing of her enemies shows her determination to see her adversaries fully punished. Having won the victory in this situation there is an uncomfortable tendency for her to want to go too far, of seeking revenge that was not necessary. The point had been made, the Jews were safe, but she had a desire for a complete conquest of those who had threatened her people. This is understandable from a perspective of her time but does not reflect so well on our so far perfect heroine.

The background to the
festival of Purim (9:18-32)

From the final section of this chapter the origins of the Jewish festival of Purim are explained and the reasons for the regional variation in its celebration. On the thirteenth and the fourteenth days of the month of Adar the Jews had assembled in the cities to punish those who had threatened and violated them. This was originally to be just the thirteenth day but as we have seen earlier in the chapter it is explained that Esther had requested an additional day of retribution, which Xerxes granted, to complete their retaliation against those guilty of heinous crimes against the Jews.

It is an interesting method of retribution – limiting to just one day the punishment meted out. Although it sounds as though it is open to considerable abuse with guilty parties going absent for twenty-four hours to avoid their punishment, it meant that an issue was dealt with and finished, rather than the ongoing sniping and wrangling that continues to take place in our communities today. There is something to be said for a system where a benevolent dictator has the power to deal with fractured social relations in a radical way and offer a fresh start to communities who have a history of problems.

Northern Ireland, Kosovo and all the other arenas of social and political unrest would be transformed if all the retribution were over and done with in one day. However, any political system has weaknesses and is only ever as good as the people who lead and work within it. We know that even with the carrying out of retribution on one day tensions between Jews and Gentiles continued. Democracy appears to be the system that offers least weaknesses and most potential for good although I can understand why some who are marginalised or disappointed by the capitalist policies of democracy think that other systems have their attractions.

Limiting retribution to one day is a pattern that might be considered in wider situations, such as when there is a break-down of relationships, in marriage, between parents and children, between friends or in business. One session of expressing the hurt and agreeing an equitable outcome might be more helpful than ongoing pain and sour feelings.

It would probably be a lot less stressful than the recent trend for taking every situation to court. Any legal settlement can take months or years and the process of resolving the problem can be a lot worse than the original issue.

For the urban Jews, dealing with their enemies took two days, so they celebrated and feasted on the fifteenth day of Adar. The rural Jews did not require a second day for settling old scores and so they feasted and celebrated on the fourteenth day.

From that time, the festival of Purim has been celebrated by the Jews. The celebration is an annual reminder of God's faithfulness in saving them from their enemies and in particular Haman. Every year the Jews were instructed to feast and celebrate the fact that their mourning and sorrow was turned to joy and celebration. It was called Purim as a play on words. It was Haman who had cast the Pur, a kind of die, as he plotted the destruction of the Jews. And yet that pur had rebounded on him and he had lost his own life rather than the Jews losing theirs.

Down the centuries the festival of Purim has continued to be important and significant. Pageants and parades are held based on the story. The story is read accompanied by boos and cheers in appropriate places. In current celebration of Purim, a festival meal takes place that lasts late into the night; mourning and sadness is forbidden. The

Talmud, the ancient Jewish commentary on the Old Testament, said this of the meal that was eaten at Purim: 'Drink wine until you can no longer distinguish between "Blessed be Mordecai and Cursed be Haman".'[11] Those Jews knew a thing or two about celebration. The festival of Purim kindles memories of God's faithfulness in protecting and providing for His people.

We have much greater reason for celebration even than Purim. We haven't just been saved from Haman but from sin, Satan and hell. When we celebrate, we celebrate a God who gives us so much – His grace is so generous and his blessings so abundant. Does the world out there see us as a celebrating people? I fear not, they see us much more in terms of formality, musty image, negativism. We should have an image as a people who have celebration at the heart of our lives together, as we are daily thankful to God for all his goodness to us.

When we visited Romania in 1989 our first impressions were of a country that was grey and colourless. The people appeared repressed having struggled to cope with years of difficulty and decades of scraping by. The buildings, the social infrastructure spoke of a society that had little to celebrate or enjoy. There was a tinge of sadness and depression to all that we saw. The sun was shining and we enjoyed hot summer days but there was hardly any evidence of the fun and entertainment that might have been expected in a European city. No street jugglers or acts, few people smiling or excited and an absence of cheerful flowers and colour. Everything was characterised by drabness. However, when we met up with Christian friends, what a difference. Never have I come across such a sense of fun and mischief. So much laughter and humour, they were like diamonds in the dirt. They had a spirit of celebration about all they did. Life was tough, very tough, with all kinds of physical deprivations and difficulties but the overriding context was of thankfulness to a God who was not limited to the short term problems, but who gave them an eternal perspective.

12

Final Thoughts

Esther chapter 10

As the book began, so it ends, with a focus on Xerxes. The start of the book was an introduction to Xerxes' wealth and success. The concluding verses bring a note of harsh realism as to the source of that prosperity. The king's wealth was gained at the expense of hundreds of thousands of others who were conscripted, required to pay heavy taxes or forced into a kind of slave labour.

The lands of the sea mentioned here are the Eastern Mediterranean islands and coastal areas which were a rich source of various goods for those who conquered them. They would be required to send in tribute, a huge proportion of their production and farming and particularly items specific to that area.

Provinces were required to support the king and his vast courts, supplying all his needs and often leaving the lands and people impoverished. It is a constant surprise that so many of the big issues of the last three millennia remain the same today. It is not difficult in our contemporary world to find impoverished people whose lives are made all the harsher because of unjust demands to support a central bureaucracy, defence system and military structure. Over \$2 billion dollars a day is spent on arms production. This is a phenomenal figure when there are so many who exist at a subsistence level. Countries like North Korea have ground the population down with wide-scale malnutrition to maintain a military system and a dictatorial central government. Cuba also, where there are enormous welfare problems to be addressed, invests enormous amounts in armaments and in a huge central bureaucracy.

The saying goes, 'The only thing that we learn from History is that we never learn'. How true that seems, although we can possibly claim some progress in that not all rulers are now able to rule despotically. There are areas of the world where there is an accountability of rulers and a fairer system of allocating resources than there once was. No system will be perfect because it is made up of people who are fallen and sinful, but the move towards democracy does give a greater sense of justice in government and equity in the way a country is organised.

In the second verse, reference is made to the Annals of the kings of the Medes and the Persians which recorded so much of the history of the court of the period. Unfortunately these documents are not available to us, having been lost in the tides of history. It would have been a huge benefit to read about Mordecai and his role as second to Xerxes. We must settle for what we can glean from the few words at the end of the book of Esther.

Mordecai had great power and authority and he was popular with the people – an unlikely combination in a politician we might think. He used his power and his position for the good of others. It is not stated but we can presume that his Jewish faith gave him a commitment to justice, righteousness and the welfare of the needy that was unique amongst Persian politicians, leaders and bureaucrats.

Mordecai's leadership had beneficial effects all round. The Jewish community was secure and prospering and the effect on the wider society was an increased quality of life – what economists call the trickle-down effect.

The brief conclusion to the Book of Esther shows an economy of words taking the readers beyond the immediate events of the deliverance of the Jews, to Mordecai's role as head of the Civil Service. It is a positive note on which to end the book, despite its brevity, showing how God's intervention on behalf of His people works to everyone's advantage. When society is under laws and values emanating from a godly perspective then it can only do good for all.

Concluding Reflections

Secular Jews in a land of exile

As we look back over the book of Esther a number of themes can be highlighted. One of these themes is of God's inclusive intentions and purposes. The story reinforces how he wants to use everyone in his plan for humankind. There is a special focus in Esther on those in a secular role being used to fulfil his intentions. As was previously mentioned, God is not named once throughout the whole book which shows the secular context of all of the events. Moreover Esther and Mordecai are not religious leaders. Much of the rest of the Old Testament is about prophets, priests and kings in their roles representing God to his people, acting as his intermediaries. But it is different here. Not only are Esther and Mordecai not religious leaders, they are also exiles, people who are not in the holy city of Jerusalem and therefore in the view of most devout Jews – they were on the edge of Jewish life. There would have been an unspoken view that to be in God's will you needed to be in Jerusalem at the centre of religious life. There was a conflict between the Zealots who had returned to Jerusalem and those who had not. The Zealots were condescending towards those who were either unable to return or chose to remain amongst Gentiles.

One of the purposes of Esther was to show that God had a plan and a high calling for secular Jews. In an age where there were tensions in the Jewish community this book is a response, defending the value and significance of those in society doing God's will without a religious label. There was a hierarchy amongst Jews in the fifth century BC. Priests in Jerusalem were holier than ordinary Jews in Jerusalem who were holier than Jews who stayed in their land of exile. The Book of Esther shows the nonsense of this and gives the clear message that all are valuable and important to God.

In the twenty-first century UK we have hierarchies in the church. It goes something like this[12]:

- *Missionaries*

They are top of the hierarchy provided they are serving God somewhere not economically developed and there is no supermarket around. These are the people who have obviously given up everything to serve God and are worthy of special acclaim. However, if they are in the Seychelles or Hawaii, then that sounds like a holiday so they go down the hierarchy a few rungs.

- *Ministers*

You have to be quite holy to be a minister because you get paid so little. There is clearly a lot of sacrifice and commitment involved in this, being available to everyone all the time. So this role has high spiritual status.

• *Deacons and elders*

These are spiritual people who are dedicated; offering service to the church. They are seen publicly serving at communion, leading in prayer and being nice to everyone, even the people the rest of us find it hard to be nice to. They are always at the prayer meeting and therefore have to have reached a high point on the holiness scale.

• *Teachers and health workers*

These people are holy because they are in a caring role. They have vocations and there are special days in church such as Hospital Sunday and Education Sunday which shows that on the ladder of sanctification they are up a number of rungs.

• *Poor Christians*

They are much holier than rich Christians. People are not quite sure why but somehow being poor seems better, which is why Christian workers are kept poor to keep them close to God.

• *Rich Christians*

Not too many brownie points in being rich as far as the holiness scale is concerned. We have a strange notion that we cannot be wealthy and holy. A view born more out of envy than truth I suspect.

- *Private sector workers*

Low on the sanctification scale are those working for profit who wallow in the world of 'filthy lucre'.

- *Journalists, Accountants, Tax Collectors, Estate Agents*

At the bottom of the holiness heap are those who are currently out of popular favour for whatever reason.

It is of course not true that there is a scale of holiness like the one above. It is a subconscious result of our warped thinking and poor grasp of God's plan for his people.

The book of Esther can help us to try and combat such misguided thinking. God has a purpose and use for all of us, whether we have religious and holy titles or whether we have a seemingly secular role. Wherever God has placed us He wants us to be His ambassadors. With neighbours, colleagues, family and friends God has a role for us to serve his purposes. We have this strange idea that it is somehow only those with special status or labels that God can use, that just as the Jews thought that you had to be in Jerusalem to serve His purposes, so we think that you have to be someone special or be somewhere appropriate.

Recently I was at a dinner for Christian business people. There were 130 people committed to using their work place as a platform for serving Christ. Their approach at work, in all of their negotiations and management of staff or working practices was based on being God's people in the work place. Their role is as crucial as any missionary or minister to the progress of the Kingdom of God. Their job titles may not sound very spiritual but the way they live their lives sanctifies their working life and makes them ministers of the Gospel in the field of commerce. They use their influence and their relationships for Christ – that is their main purpose and the overriding objective in all they do.

In our churches we need to take much more seriously our responsibility to send each other out in ministry every week to whatever situation God has put us in. We fail to see the context in which we live out our daily lives as God's opportunity to use us as a channel for his power.

The silent hand of God

The second theme on which to focus further is recognising God at work in hidden ways and in the endless routines of our lives. As our society appears to be further and further removed from a Christian basis and is increasingly secular in its structures, values and institutions, the Book of Esther is a reminder not to lose hope and not to lose a vision of God at work. The Persian Empire was an alien culture for Jewish people, it was not a community in which God's presence was readily felt and in which belief in Him and commitment to Him was widely acknowledged. That did not mean God's plans were thwarted and that His purposes were not being worked out. The Book of Esther gives us cause for optimism in the most difficult situations to have confidence in. God has not abandoned His objectives and He is achieving His plan in all circumstances.

'God moves in mysterious ways his wonders to perform,'[13] as the popular old hymn puts it. Our expectation of God is often so narrow and stereotyped. So limited to religious ways of doing things forgetting that our God is the great Creator who is more imaginative, innovative and creative than we can imagine. In situations where we might give up or compromise or consider hopeless, God is at work. His silent hand is moving in ways that we might not recognise until eternity.

You may feel at this current time that you are somehow exiled from God's activity, God's work and God's blessing. As Esther and Mordecai were exiled from Jerusalem and the centre of worship so it feels as if God is blessing elsewhere but somehow you are excluded from it. You wait to hear God's voice as others speak so confidently about God's leading and guidance, His intervention and activity. You look to see Him at work in your community and life but He seems so strangely silent.

The eyes of faith see God at work not in the obvious manifestations but in the apparently ungodly unfolding of events. Where no mention of God is made, where there is little evidence of his activity, it is in this unpromising context God is moving and fulfilling his purposes.

I have mentioned Romania already in this book – let me return to it again. I remember a year before President Ceasescu was toppled, Nic Geoghita, an anaesthetist and pastor from Oradea, was preaching in the UK. Romania appeared a godforsaken land with Christians facing opposition and harassment on a daily basis. There was little evidence of God at work in the political and social structure. Nic, as he preached, commented that the Romanians were preparing to celebrate forty years of Communism in their land in the following year and that they were all getting excited about that. Nic looked at the audience and said with a mischievous twinkle in his eye, 'they don't realise how significant forty years is to God. Forty years is the time of liberation, the time for freedom.' His meaning was clear – he expected that forty years would mark not a celebration of Communism but the defeat of Communism and the liberation of God's people. I remember thinking that this was great rhetoric, great dreams, but the evidence for it happening was not promising. And yet eighteen months later the Berlin wall came down and freedom spread across Eastern Europe including Romania.

God had appeared to be silent. There was no clear evidence of God at work, but his purposes were being fulfilled on the world stage in ways that could not have been planned by human minds alone. When God seems silent it may be because we have turned down the volume without realising what we've done.

Human responsibility and God's Sovereignty

A third issue raised by the book of Esther is the old prickly question of the paradox of human involvement and initiative and God's omnipotence in all situations. There is a stress in the Book of Esther on human responsibility and there is a conviction presented that God's people should take the initiative and act with integrity and courage and take risks when necessary. This is, however, in the context of the belief that God is sovereign and He acts supremely to fulfil His purposes, overriding our puny efforts to do what is right. The Book of Esther is a marvellous record of God acting on behalf of his people, but that must not lead us to presume on God. Esther and her people never presumed to know God's will but did what was right according to the measure of understanding they had been given.

No-one should presume on God. He acted to save the Jews in the time of Esther but we cannot therefore assume that he will act in the same way on other occasions. We should be awed at His willingness to intervene on our behalf when we are such weak and failing individuals. But there are many episodes when it appears that God has not rescued his people, at Masada for example in AD73 when 960 Jews assumed God would save them from the siege by the Romans. They were not saved and so committed suicide to avoid a worse fate from the Romans. Then there is the Holocaust in Germany. We may ask why did these things happen and we may not get an answer that we can grasp. Yet God does overrule in a myriad of ways. The fall of the Berlin Wall, the success of Dunkirk, the end of apartheid were all events that had been prayed for and sought from God. The daily acts of God's providence in individual believers' lives build up to a technicolour picture of God intervening generously and willingly.

Fasting and feasting

The fourth theme to give additional attention to is that of feasting and fasting. Feast occurs twenty times in Esther and only twenty-four times in the rest of the Old Testament which certainly indicates a focus and an emphasis not found in other Biblical material. Fasting is not mentioned as much but it is of key significance in the book. Scholars who have studied the structure of Esther have suggested that there is a masterly use of the feasts and fasts as both a contrast and a way to give a framework to the events.

The events begin with banquets, Xerxes' celebration of his success, Vashti's separate women's banquet and the banquet for Esther when she is made queen. There are also the banquets that Esther initiates for Xerxes and Haman and the book concludes with the feasting surrounding Purim. The fasting highlights and contrasts with the theme of feasting, for Esther there is an irony that she goes immediately from fasting and praying to God to feasting with Xerxes and Haman.

What are we to make of all of this? Feasting is an essential feature of human life – it is the best context for commemoration, bargaining, negotiation, celebration and decision making. We have already commented earlier that for the Jews celebration was a crucial feature of their recognition of God's faithfulness. In middle eastern culture a meal was essential for social interaction, a chance to be hospitable, to make the guests feel significant and valued. Over a meal people are more relaxed and therefore more able to discuss and be flexible, to be open- minded and responsive to new ideas. I wonder whether in our fast food society we are losing many opportunities for the discussions and social transactions that could take place over a long meal. By our emphasis on speed, on eating on the run and on not having time to be hospitable we send signals that people don't matter to us, that they are not important enough for us to take time with and not significant enough for us to give up our agenda for them.

Berg[14] has highlighted the link between feasting and power. The feasts 'in honour of Haman' were actually feasts plotting his downfall and therefore his disempowering, the feast of the women at the beginning of the events led to the disempowering of Vashti but Purim celebrates the empowerment of the Jews and is a commemoration of their change of fortune.

The opposite side of feasting is of course fasting; a matter of self-denial, sacrificing food for a day for God. The book of Esther does not present fasting as an activity which gains merit, it is not a case that the fasting itself is of virtue. The words of the prophet spell this out clearly in Isaiah 58:3-12 'Yet on the day of your fasting, you do as you please and exploit all your workers. Your fasting ends in quarrelling and strife, and in striking each other with wicked fists. You cannot fast as you do today and expect your voice to be heard on high.' Fasting alone is of no value; it is only when it leads to justice and godly living that it has worth.

This focus in Esther raises the question of whether Christians should feast or fast. The Messiah has come and we should celebrate all that signifies and means. And yet we are also living in the midst of a spiritual battle, where the war has been won and there are various battles still going on. It would be naïve of anyone to think that being a Christian makes life one long celebration. There is still a need for fasting as a discipline to focus clearly on issues that are faced. It is an act of sacrifice showing to God and ourselves that we are intent on giving a situation our time and energy.

Obedience and disobedience

A further issue that is revealed in Esther is that of obedience and disobedience. Again I am indebted to Berg[14] for her insights into this motif. Vashti was disobedient to Xerxes, Esther was obedient to Mordecai, Hegai and Xerxes. Mordecai obeyed Esther (Esther 4:17) but disobeyed Haman. Haman was disobedient through presumption. In presuming to know the royal will in his plans to destroy the Jews he disobeyed the wishes of the emperor and he presumed the royal will in erecting gallows on which to punish Mordecai, which was an act of disobedience against the king. Esther was disobedient as far as protocol was concerned when she entered the king's presence uninvited (5:1-5).

Only the disobedience of Esther and Mordecai yield favourable results. They disobey and in so doing put themselves at personal risk. Their civil disobedience for their cause is not to be equated with a disregard for the law. The concept of law is taken seriously but even greater store is laid on the individual's commitment to the spiritual community: the law does not take precedence over that.

157

Knowing the consequences and punishments that might follow an act of disobedience, a faithful Jew must at times disobey the law and sacrifice personal safety when required to do so by the spiritual requirements of religion and conscience.

As Christians we are called to uphold and recognise the value of the law and yet there may be times when as an act of civil disobedience we would need to protest or break the law in order to obey a higher calling. It is a decision that should not be taken lightly and there is no room for complaint when the full force of the law bears down on Christian law breakers. There is a certain naivety around that makes some think that God will protect them from punishment if they make a stand against the law and for the Gospel and they are surprised or infuriated when they find they are being punished for standing by their conscience. We may need to break the law and we may find ourselves punished for it, but if it is God's will he gives his protection and can see us through. The words of Peter and John in Acts 4:19 remind us of our final authority: 'Judge for yourselves whether it is right in God's sight to obey you rather than God.'

Mordecai and Esther respected the law but when they found the law was compromising their beliefs and conscience they were willing to take the risk of a severe punishment for breaking the law and drawing attention to the issue of their people's unjust sentence of death. So too, we should be people who honour and obey the law as a routine matter but when there are exceptional circumstances we must be prepared to disobey the law in order to obey what we believe is God's leading.

Indestructibility of the Jews

There is in the book of Esther a reminder that the Jews are a special people, that they are God's special people and for that reason alone they will survive, they could not be wiped out by Haman, Hitler or any other enemy. In 6:13, Haman's wife and advisers comment that Haman cannot succeed against Mordecai. Mordecai's genealogy (2:5-6) signifies the survival of the Jews despite captivity and exile. As a nation their indestructibility is emphasised.

This has been confirmed in recent history with the establishment of the state of Israel against all the odds and the durability of the race despite the fact that over the centuries so much has been against them.

And finally Esther

At the end of our reflections on Esther there are some final points to be made. I hope like me you have found it a challenging and captivating book that makes the most of suspense, intrigue and humour. It is a human book and by that I mean it is a story that shows all the best that people are capable of, and the worst. It shows our potential for good and our appalling potential for evil. It portrays the danger of taking yourself too seriously, of thinking you are so important that you are above normal human weaknesses, and of not being able to recognise situations for what they are. There is a lot spoken today of emotional intelligence, of being able to respond in the most beneficial way to people, and of being able to recognise and take risks when appropriate. Esther and Mordecai, apart from being godly people, are both emotionally intelligent people who handle every circumstance in the best way. Haman is the complete opposite. An emotionally challenged individual, he shows no sensitivity to others or to circumstances; his agenda is the only one he recognises and he is unable to read the signals of events accurately. We focus so much today on qualifications and academic achievement when what will help us far more is emotional insights or perhaps, in old-fashioned terminology common sense and wisdom.

Despite all the scholars and learned people who think that Esther should not be in the Bible, I am grateful that we have such a book in which God is so subtly present in all that takes place because that is how it is for the majority of us. For many, if not all of us, the days and months are made up of work and family life, of births, weddings and funerals, without God explicitly being there and intervening. That doesn't mean that He isn't, it is just that the hidden workings of God are not always seen by our clouded vision. Esther gives us hope that in all that goes on God is working and moving in ways that we cannot imagine. Who would think that a sleepless night would be the pivot on which the fortune of Haman foundered?

So many human themes are raised in the book that it can almost be a handbook for sensible living. The topics covered include:

- Knowing when not to compromise
- Raising children
- Being teachable
- Willingness to obey those you have taught
- Pride
- Presumption
- Taking risks
- Loyalty
- Arrogance
- Modesty
- Power
- Objective advice
- Power and impotence
- Weakness
- Judging human nature
- Revenge
- Celebration

So many issues that face us day by day in our ordinary routines and give us examples of how we can learn from others' mistakes and successes. I fear I have not done justice to the rich seam of God's truth found in the brief ten chapters of Esther and yet I hope your spiritual appetite has been sufficiently whetted so you might continue to reflect upon this stunning story and so be fed further.

A final thought is how the Book of Esther entertains us with serendipity, that delightfully unexpected outcome to events; defined by one wit as when a young man went into a library to take out a book and instead took out the librarian. Against all the odds, expecting to save their people at the most, Esther and Mordecai discover themselves enjoying the full extent of the king's favour. When they might have faced death they faced life at its richest.

However, there is another side to Esther and that is the reversal of human expectations defined in Aristotle's Poetics as peripety.[15] This is when events produce the opposite of what is expected and cause considerable frustration to hopes, dreams and ambitions. Just when things were going well for Esther and Mordecai, along came Haman. Just when things were going well for Haman, along came Mordecai. Life is full of frustrations – things not working out as we think they should – of disappointment and disillusionment leading to disaffection. The message of Esther to all of us who face the uncertainties of daily life and feel somehow that life always lets us down and never delivers on its promises is that God's justice triumphs despite the frustration and reversal of expectations. For all the things that don't work out as we would like them to and seem weighted against us there is a message that despite the minor irritations and the major disappointments, God is in control and he is the winner in all things.

13

The Greek Additions to the
Hebrew Text of Esther

The book of Esther which is found in the NIV or
other common translations of the Bible is taken from
the Masoretic text which is an ancient Hebrew
version of the Scripture. Other texts exist from a
later period written in Greek which contain additional
verses enlarging the original narrative. There are
167 Hebrew verses and added to this are 107 verses
in the Greek text. The Greek additions, while
interesting in the insight they give, are more fanciful
and less convincing than the Hebrew text alone.
They are not convincing in their portrayal of the
characters although it is intriguing to understand
how others have viewed and sought to interpret
the book of Esther. In the Jerusalem Bible the Greek
additions are included with some sections also in
the Apocrypha.

Mordecai's dream
The Greek text has an additional introduction which
is a dream of Mordecai. It is written in the style of
an apocalyptic vision putting the conflict between
Mordecai and Haman on to a cosmic scale. It is
presented as more than just a political struggle or

an issue of discrimination and genocide but a battle in the heavenly realms between good and evil, with God's people overpowering their opponents.

In this section there is a more detailed and colourful account of the uncovering of the conspiracy to assassinate Xerxes by Bigthana and Teresh. There is mention of their torture and execution and comment, at this early stage, on Mordecai's elevation to a place of importance. The introduction concludes with a comment on Haman, that he was determined to injure Mordecai because of what had happened to Bigthana and Teresh. This gives an explanation for the excessive actions of Haman against Mordecai later and may imply that Haman was not the loyal servant that Xerxes thought, but would support whoever it seemed in his best interest to support at the time.

Xerxes' letter

The second Greek addition is details of the letter that went out in Xerxes' name to all of the provinces explaining the punishment to be meted out on the Jews. The letter speaks of Haman as 'one eminent among us for prudence and well proved for his unfailing devotion and unshakeable trustworthiness, and in rank second only to our majesty'. The Jews are not named but are described as 'a certain ill-disposed people, opposed by its laws to every other nation and continually defying the royal ordinances, in such a way as to obstruct that form of government assured by us to the general good'. It goes on to say: 'this people, unique of its kind, is in complete opposition to all mankind from which it differs by its outlandish system of laws, that it is hostile to our interests and that it commits the most heinous crimes, to the point of endangering the stability of the realm.'

This perversion of the facts about Jewish Law and the hysterical manner in which it is written does help to explain how Haman could mobilise the whole empire against the Jews. It is not so different from language used today of groups who are distinctive, people who stand out and through no fault of their own, attract a variety of vicious accusations against them to the effect that they are a danger to society and to what is good.

Mordecai's prayer

This is an attempt by a later writer to give a more religious slant to the book. The prayers are credible in some ways but lack an authentic ring. It is obviously the over-eager contribution of an editor wanting to increase Mordecai's spiritual image in a clumsy and unsubtle manner. The Mordecai portrayed in the Masoretic text would have been unlikely to say to God as he defends himself in prayer: 'You know that no insolence, arrogance, vainglory prompted me to this.' This lacks the modest integrity that we have seen in Mordecai in his other actions.

Esther's prayer

When Esther realised what she had to do to save her people, she is horrified and despairing. This section of the Greek text seeks to give an insight into her response to the situation and her desperate prayer to God. Esther is described as 'humbling her body severely' and 'she covered her head with ashes and dung'. This is all an attempt to reinforce the reader's understanding of the appalling situation she is in and how she is inadequate to deal with it.

The prayer is a statement of God's sovereign power and God's promise to His people through all generations. The prayer begs God to act on behalf of her people and to bring justice for them.

For a later editor of this book this passage with others seeks to redeem the book from being merely a secular story, with little theology and spiritual significance, to a narrative which gives much greater focus on religious matters. It seems to add what some might consider to be missing.

Esther's approach to the king

There is interwoven with the original account of Esther's approach to the king a more detailed and spiritual explanation of events. God is explicitly mentioned and Esther's condition after praying and fasting for three days is shown. She is described as leaning 'on the maid's arm as though languidly, but in fact because her body was too weak to support her'. It further states that while 'her face radiated joy and love ... her heart shrank with fear'. When Xerxes first saw Esther standing there without having been invited 'he looked on her, blazing with anger... God changed the king's heart, inducing a milder spirit.'

This section may have been close to the truth but we have no way of knowing – like most commentators it is a helpful insight but it would be unwise to build any further teaching on it.

Mordecai's letter

This letter was dictated by Mordecai and was inserted into chapter 8. It explained Haman as a traitor to the empire and concluded that it was all part of a conspiracy on Haman's part to hand the Persian empire over to the Macedonians. Since Haman had no Persian blood in him and had acted against those who had treated him so well, this interpretation was persuasive.

The letter ends in a way which ensures the protection of the Jews and is worded in the form of a threat. 'Every city and generally every country, which does not follow these instructions, will be mercilessly devastated with fire and sword, and made not only inaccessible to men but hateful to wild animals and birds for ever.' It is not surprising if this was close to what was actually written that so many Gentiles became Jews for fear of them (8:17).

Mordecai's conclusion about his dream
The additional texts finish with Mordecai commenting on his dream and how it has been fulfilled. It is an explicit statement of Jewish victory over all of the nations of the world and is again portrayed in an apocalyptic style. It does not fit easily with the rest of the book and is more of an interpretation by those who wanted more theological substance or to defend it against those who could not see any value in it.

Variety of Esther texts
The variations on Esther in the manuscripts that are available show something of the process involved in developing the canon of Scripture. The variations highlight the differing views people have had about Esther and the different emphases that have been drawn out of this surprising story. It is my view that the variations strengthen the argument for Esther as a historical book, since historical documents have often been tampered with and the process of excluding some sections as later additions gives us greater confidence in the book as part of God's word for his people.

Using the Study Guide

Hints for small group leaders

• If possible encourage the group members to have read the chapter from 'A True First Lady' prior to the small group.

• Begin the session with prayer seeking the guidance and leading of the Holy Spirit.

• Read together the chapter of Esther which you will be studying.

• Before looking at the questions take a few moments to ask the group what their immediate response to the chapter is. For example: *Does anything particular strike them? Does one verse stand out? Is there anything they don't understand? What is the main theme of the chapter?*

• Use the questions as a tool and support and **don't** be mastered by them. They are to help you in your discussion. Don't feel that you have to answer all the questions. If an important issue arises that you want the group to discuss and develop then have the confidence to ignore some of the published questions.

• Conclude the study by sharing what the teaching of the chapter has meant personally and how as a group you will seek to live it out in the coming week.

• Begin the next session with a brief reflection on what was learnt previously and how it has been relevant or reinforced in the intervening time.

When Bible Study in groups is tough for whatever reason remember the words of Deuteronomy 32:47 'These are not just idle words for you - they are your life.'

Study questions for small groups

Esther chapter 1 (What a party!)

1. Can a story from so many centuries ago and from such a different cultural context have anything to say to us today? How?

2. Vashti's behaviour (verse 16) is considered wrong and damaging to the whole Persian nation. There was a fear that all women would follow her example and that there would be an absence of respect and an undermining of domestic relationships.
In the light of the society in which she lived do you think that Vashti was wrong to take a stand against her husband in such a public way- was she a heroine or a fool? What alternative action could she have taken?

3. Have you ever had to take a stand as a matter of conscience or principle of faith which is contrary to the law or prevailing values?

4. When are Christians today compelled to follow the example of Peter (Acts 4:19-20) and obey God rather than the ruling authorities?

5. Most often we find ourselves in situations that are not clear. How do you know when it is right to

make a stand on an issue and when not to? (Jas. 1:5 might help).

6. It is in the secular context of an ungodly king and a raucous royal court that God is working out his purposes. Does this surprise, encourage or concern you?

7. As you reflect on your own situation and the wider national and political context - do you perceive God moving amongst the ungodly and using them for his purposes?

8. Alcohol and over-indulgence seem to have been central factors in this situation of moral impropriety when Vashti was ordered to parade before her husband and his friends. Could we argue from this evidence and the abuse of alcohol in our own society that the most helpful and distinctive lifestyle choice for Christians is to be teetotal?

Esther chapter 2 (Miss Persia 487BC)

1. Mordecai brought Esther up with clear values and a strong sense of right and wrong. She had integrity and a firm religious identity. He did this as a single man without the community support that might have helped him. Is the example of Mordecai's parenting skills an important model for parents today?

2. Why might it be more difficult today than in Mordecai's time for parents to bring up their children successfully?

3. Do Christian parents focus adequately on spiritual values or are they too readily sucked into the expectations and values around them of success, achievement and selfish ambition?

4. Esther is presented in this chapter as a young woman of wisdom and humility. She listened to advice and accepted the counsel of others and did not seek to take credit undeservedly. Reflect on your past experience and consider whether you yourself or those around you have been willing to accept the advice and counsel of others. How far have you or others benefited from this?

5. Working as a team and being prepared to share 'the glory' with others is an important aspect of life in our current world. Share examples of when this has happened effectively or when someone has selfishly and unjustly claimed the credit for themselves. Describe the consequences of these examples.

6. Why can it never be right for a follower of Jesus Christ to take all the credit for the success of a project?

7. What is it about both Esther and Mordecai that made them so usable by God? What aspect of their characters do we find it hardest to imitate?

8. Who are the role models today? Those with character, authentic heroes who model faith and integrity?

Esther chapter 3 (The Maggot in the Cherry Pie)

1. We are introduced to Haman as an unpleasant individual. He was an Agagite whose philosophy of life was that all that happened did so by chance. What motivated and drove Haman?

2. Why was Haman so incensed by the actions of Mordecai?

3. Can you identify the main flaw in Haman's character?

4. Mordecai refused to bow to Haman. He would not give inappropriate honour to a traditional enemy of the Jewish people whose character and behaviour was abhorrent. Are there Haman type figures around today? Examples?

5. How should we respond to their excessive demands for respect or honour?

6. If we do not take a stand against those who abuse their position and authority, what are the likely consequences?

7. It seems outrageous to our contemporary minds that Haman could so easily plan the annihilation of a whole race of people. Genocide, a word that has been in common usage recently, is sadly not a recent phenomenon. Why is genocide such an evil?

8. What are the causes of genocide today?

9. King Xerxes accepts all that Haman says to him without questioning or debate. How does this chapter of Esther present Xerxes? In what ways is he a poor leader?

10. In the light of Xerxes' example of flawed leadership should we be more meticulous in fulfilling our responsibilities to pray for those in authority?

Esther chapter 4 (Sackcloth and Ashes)

1. The terror of the situation that the Jewish people found themselves in is unimaginable. The nightmare of thinking that you and your family will be destroyed is too appalling to consider. They had been through so much already and it must have seemed unfair to face further catastrophe. Would it have been

appropriate for the Jewish people to have complained to God that their situation was unfair and they shouldn't have to face yet another crisis?

2. Why do you think that down the centuries the Jews have been the victims of such prejudice and discrimination?

3. Esther did not know what was going on, yet was aware of Mordecai's distress. Further, she was not fully experienced in the ways and protocol of the court. She was isolated and poorly equipped for her role. Is her crucial role in these events a reminder that God can use us and others when we appear to lack the experience, confidence or qualifications needed? Can this be an encouragement or a worry for us?

4. Mordecai's role in this chapter is critical. He responded to the despair of the situation by wailing and wearing sackcloth and ashes. He also shows himself to be a man of great faith. How do we respond to crises and grief? Is the stiff upper lip still encouraged and is it helpful? Would we cope better in the long term if we had the twenty-first Century equivalent of sackcloth and ashes and wailing?

5. Why is Mordecai's comment in verse 14, 'relief

and deliverance for the Jews will arise', a statement of faith? Compare it to Job 19:25; Acts 7:59-60. In times of despair are you able to echo the words of Mordecai, Job and Stephen?

6. Esther's response to the tragedy is exemplary. She did not shut herself away from the problem as she might have been tempted to do. Her request that others join her in prayer and fasting shows her reliance on God. She knew what she needed to do but she had no idea of how it would end. Have you ever had the feeling that God has put you into a particular circumstance or role 'for such a time as this'?

7. Who do we turn to in a crisis? Is prayer and/or fasting our automatic reaction?

8. Following the leading of the Holy Spirit can at times mean consequences are uncertain and the future potentially difficult. Are we tempted to think that being obedient to Christ should mean a life of peace and comfort? See Acts 21:10-14.

Esther chapter 5 (Diplomacy, tact and dignity)

1. Esther is masterful in her display of tact and diplomacy as she plans and executes her strategy to save her people. Can you think of occasions when

a difficult situation has been made worse by a well-intentioned but tactless and ungracious person?

2. Consider Matthew 10:16, 'therefore be as shrewd as snakes and as innocent as doves' and suggest how far Esther fulfils it. Is this verse applicable in our situations today?

3. As the immense power and influence of Haman unfolds before us it becomes evident that he is ill-equipped for such responsibility and privilege. What should we look for in potential leaders to ensure that the influence and power they exercise is used effectively and with integrity?

4. Haman is eaten up by anger and bitterness despite all the success of his life. Suggest ways in which we can avoid such attitudes.(Romans 12:9-21)

5. Is it a pattern today for people to be destroyed by jealousy and anger?

6. It is most likely that Haman was an intelligent and skilful person to achieve such a high position yet he lacked basic wisdom and listened to biased friends and family. Discuss both the negative and positive influence of family friends and suggest the kind of relationships we need when considering important decisions.

Esther chapter 6 (The Silent Hand of God)

1. It appeared that God was silent and inactive as events move forward. However, he was at work even in Xerxes' insomnia. How is this evidence of God's secret hand an encouragement in our difficulties today?

2. Haman, in his arrogance and pride, immediately jumped to wrong conclusions (6:6). How might the advice of Proverbs 3:5-6 and 11:2 help us not to do the same?

3. Mordecai might have expected earlier recognition of his action in saving the King's life, chapter 2:21-23. There was a delay in him receiving his reward. How could this understanding that things don't always follow our preferred time-scale help us to cope with the disappointment of delays and seeming lack of recognition?

4. Mordecai had every reason to push himself forward after the King had so publicly honoured him but he remained modest. Reflect on what Jesus says about a humble attitude in the parable of the wedding feast Luke 14:7-11.

5. How far is this teaching the opposite of how people behave today?

6. The chapter ends with what the evil Haman had done rebounding on him. Galatians 6:7 'God cannot be mocked, a person reaps what he sows' is illustrated by Haman but is it true today? Don't many people seem to get away with it? They may sow selfishly and arrogantly but reap prosperity.

Esther chapter 7 (Hoisted on his own Petard)

1. Esther's approach to the King is respectful. She honours his authority as King and is modest in her manner. Should we as God's people follow her example when approaching:
(a) community leaders such as an MP, mayor or member of the royal family?
(b) the King of Kings, the Lord God?

2. At this critical stage of events Esther shows remarkable courage and wisdom. Suggest occasions when you might particularly need both courage and wisdom. Does James 1:5 give you insight into how to face such situations?

3. I have suggested that Xerxes would have been disappointed to be betrayed by someone in whom he has put so much trust. This is not an uncommon occurrence. Are there ways that we can avoid being let down by others or should we accept it as one of the costs of living in a fallen world?

4. The temptation to gloat and revel in Haman's ghastly demise is almost irresistible. Why is it wrong? Use the following verses to help you: Romans 12:14, 17, 21

5. What are the flaws in Haman's character, that, in our most honest moments, we admit to seeing in ourselves? If you have the courage to admit your failings with others then remind yourself of 1 John 1:9.

Esther chapter 8 (It's not over 'til it's over)

1. Esther and Mordecai must have been relieved to see the end of Haman but the situation was still critical. The edict remained in force, so the annihilation of the Jews was still on the statute books. Just because a major victory had been won it did not mean that they could relax. Can you think of examples of when this is true of Christian events and activities when people are tempted not to see the job through to the end?

2. What parallels are there in Christian experience and growth? Colossians 2:7 and Philippians 2:12-13 might be of assistance.

3. Esther has been discreet about her nationality until this critical part of events. We are reminded in

8:5-6 that at this point she is open about her people and her religion. Why do you think that she has been so discreet about being Jewish?

4. Does this teach us anything about the way we present our identity as Christians to those around us?

5. It is immensely impressive that before the days of telecommunications, motorised vehicles or air transport, that the edict saving the Jews was communicated to every province in the empire so speedily.

Should such efficiency and organisation be of concern in our activities seeking to build the Kingdom of God? You might find it helpful to reflect on the organised nature of God's people seen, for example, in the book of Numbers or the spiritual gift of administration mentioned in 1 Corinthians 12:28.

6. Celebration and feasting are a key feature of this chapter (8:17) and the book of Esther as a whole, as well as being a key feature of the culture of the Ancient East and the Jewish community. They celebrated with generosity and style. Are our Christian celebrations, church teas and dinners in church halls, an adequate celebration together of being God's community?

7. When does celebration turn from being positive and good for a community to being unhelpful and damaging?

8. In 8:17 we are told that many converted to Judaism because of fear of the Jews. Is it ever likely in the twenty-first century that people would become Christians for such dubious motives?

Esther chapter 9 (Triumphant Jews)

1. This chapter shows how the Jews protected themselves from their enemies and punished those who opposed them. Does it shock you that the Jews took revenge which involved thousands being killed?

2. Why is it significant that the Jews 'did not lay hands on the plunder' (verse 16)? What does this suggest about their motivation for the slaughter?

3. Read Deuteronomy 19:21 and 32:35 and Matthew 5:38-42 and Romans 12:17-19. Compare the differences in teaching about revenge in the Old and New Testament.

4. The Jews celebrated their rescue from Haman's evil schemes with the annual festival of Purim which was a time of great joy and thanksgiving. Christians have been rescued from a much greater

threat than even Haman, we have been saved from separation from God for ever because of our sin. Reflect on how you celebrate your salvation. Does it adequately express the amazing rescue carried out by Jesus or have we become a little too familiar with our faith and forgotten its true significance?

5. Are there ways in which we could ensure that our celebration of God's rescue of us is kept fresh, sincere and genuine as a community?

Esther chapter 10 and wider issues (Esther: a post-feminist icon, and Final Thoughts)

1. Mordecai rose to the highest rank in the realm apart from the King. Why does verse 3 suggest he was so popular? Are such qualities in short supply amongst leaders today?

2. Mordecai is a great example to us in many ways but there is one perplexing issue. Why did he allow Esther to be selected for the King's harem? Why did he not hide her away and avoid such a potentially horrific fate for a girl from a Jewish family?

3. People tend to want to take sides on most issues today and even Esther has her opponents and her supporters. Those unimpressed by Esther would suggest that she submitted far too easily to an evil

and oppressive regime and that Vashti was the true heroine because she, with heroic courage, took a stand for justice. Do you think the example of Vashti is a more constructive role model for the contemporary world than the example of Esther?

References

1. B. W. Anderson 'The Book of Esther', in *IB3*. ed.G.A.Buttrick (New York/Nashville:Abingdon,1954)

2. J. Gray *Men are from Mars, Women are from Venus*, (London: HarperCollins,1993)

3. M.Parris *The Great Unfrocked: Two Thousand Years of Scanda*l (London: Robson Books Ltd, 1998)

4. J.G.Baldwin *Esther* (Leicester: IVP,1984)

5. C. Swindoll *David* (Dallas, Texas: Word Publishing Ltd, 1997)

6. *'Paranoid? We have every reason to be.'* The Sunday Times News International, 11th July 1999

7. C.S.Lewis *The Problem of Pain* (London: Harper Collins,1986)

8. C. Swindoll *Esther* (Nashville,Tennessee: Word Publishing, 1997)

9. D.N.Freedman, quoted by Moore in *Esther*, (Garden City, NY: Doubleday, 1971)

10. C.S.Lewis *Mere Christianity* (London: Harper Collins, 1997)

11. J.Bowker *The Complete Bible Handbook* (London: Dorling Kinderseley, 1998)

12. M.Greene, Idea for this hierarchy taken from unpublished presentation given at London Bible College

13. 'God moves in a mysterious way'

14. S.B.Berg *The Book of Esther: Motifs, Themes and Structure* (Missoula,Montana: Scholars Press,1979)

15. *Aristotle's Poetics* (New York: W. W. Norton & Co Ltd ,1982) cited by Berg

Christian Focus Publications publishes biblically-accurate books for adults and children. The books in the adult range are published in three imprints.

Christian Heritage contains classic writings from the past.

Christian Focus contains popular works including biographies, commentaries, doctrine, and Christian living.

Mentor focuses on books written at a level suitable for Bible College and seminary students, pastors, and others; the imprint includes commentaries, doctrinal studies, examination of current issues, and church history.

For a free catalogue of all our titles, please write to

Christian Focus Publications,
Geanies House, Fearn,
Ross-shire, IV20 1TW, Great Britain

For details of our titles visit us on our web site

http://www.christianfocus.com

BS 1375.2 .T53 1995
Tidball, Dianne.
Esther

DATE DUE

DEC 2 1 2008			

#47-0108 Peel Off Pressure Sensitive